ADOBE® FLASH® CATALYST™ CS5
CLASSROOM IN A BOOK®

The official training workbook from Adobe Systems

Adobe®

Writer: Scott Tapley
Project Editor: Rebecca Freed
Development Editor: Robyn G. Thomas
Production Editor: Cory Borman
Copyeditor: Scout Festa
Technical Editor: Angela Nimer
Compositor: David Van Ness
Indexer: James Minkin
Cover design: Eddie Yuen
Interior design: Mimi Heft

Printed and bound in the United States of America

ISBN-13:   978-0-321-70358-3
ISBN-10:   0-321-70358-8

9 8 7 6 5 4 3 2 1

WHAT'S ON THE DISC

Here is an overview of the contents of the Classroom in a Book disc

The *Adobe Flash Catalyst CS5 Classroom in a Book* disc includes the lesson files that you'll need to complete the exercises in this book, as well as other content to help you learn more about Adobe Flash Catalyst CS5 and use it with greater efficiency and ease. The diagram below represents the contents of the disc, which should help you locate the files you need.

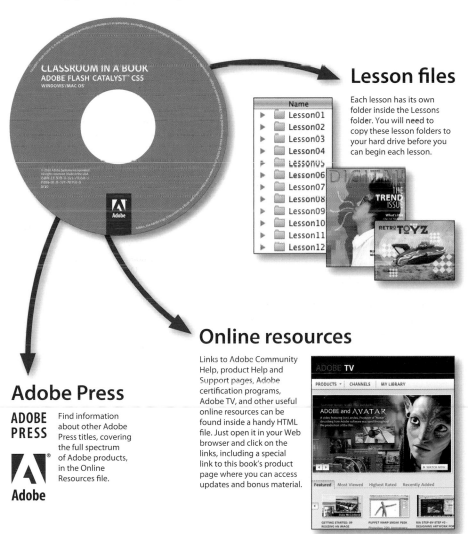

Lesson files

Each lesson has its own folder inside the Lessons folder. You will need to copy these lesson folders to your hard drive before you can begin each lesson.

Online resources

Links to Adobe Community Help, product Help and Support pages, Adobe certification programs, Adobe TV, and other useful online resources can be found inside a handy HTML file. Just open it in your Web browser and click on the links, including a special link to this book's product page where you can access updates and bonus material.

Adobe Press

Find information about other Adobe Press titles, covering the full spectrum of Adobe products, in the Online Resources file.

CONTENTS

6   CREATING INTERACTIVE COMPONENTS   **88**

11 DRAWING AND EDITING ARTWORK 196

GETTING STARTED

Flash Catalyst is a tool for designers who want to create rich application interfaces and interactive content without authoring a single line of code. Examples include interactive ads, product guides, design portfolios, microsites, data-centric rich Internet applications (RIAs), and more.

If you're familiar with other Adobe design tools, such as Photoshop, Illustrator, and Fireworks, then you're going to really like the Flash Catalyst workflow. For example, you can design the artwork for your Flash Catalyst project using Photoshop, and then import the entire design document into Flash Catalyst. Convert the artwork and other assets into interactive components, such as navigation buttons and scroll bars. Define the different states, or views, of your application. Add interactions used to transition from one page or component state to another, link to a website, or control animation, video, and sound effects. Add smooth transitions, 3D animation, and other special effects. Finally, publish your project to the web or as an Adobe AIR desktop application.

Flash Catalyst is a great tool for quickly producing interactive application prototypes using a collection of built-in wireframe components.

Flash Catalyst also allows you to work more efficiently with developers who use Adobe Flash Builder 4 (formerly Flex Builder) and the Adobe Flex 4 Software Development Kit (SDK). You design the functional user experience in Flash Catalyst and then provide the project file to developers who use Flash Builder to add additional functionality and integration with data and services.

With the introduction of Flash Catalyst, you now have complete control over the integrity of your original artwork and design vision when producing interactive content.

About Classroom in a Book

Adobe Flash Catalyst CS5 Classroom in a Book is part of the official training series for the Adobe Flash platform. The lessons are designed so that you can learn at your own pace. If you're new to Flash Catalyst, you'll learn the fundamental concepts and features you'll need to accomplish a wide range of techniques covered in the book, but also gain enough understanding of the application to be able to learn additional techniques on your own. If you've already started working with Flash Catalyst, you'll find that Classroom in a Book teaches advanced features, including tips and technique and best practices.

Although each lesson provides step-by-step instructions for completing specific skills, and each lesson builds upon the previous lessons, there is room for experimentation. You can follow the book from start to finish, or do only the lessons that match your interests and needs. Each lesson concludes with a review section summarizing what you've covered.

Prerequisites

Before you begin to use *Adobe Flash Catalyst CS5 Classroom in a Book*, make sure that your system is set up correctly and that you've installed the required software. You should know how to use the mouse and standard menus and commands, and also how to open, save, and close files. If you need to review these techniques, see the printed or online documentation included with your Microsoft Windows or Apple Mac OS software.

This book is intended for any designer who produces interactive content for the web or desktop. You will have more success with Flash Catalyst if you are already familiar with Adobe Illustrator, Adobe Photoshop, or Adobe Fireworks, and have a basic understanding of structuring artwork using layers and groups.

This book assumes no programming experience. If you are a designer wishing to learn Flash Catalyst, but perhaps are a little daunted by code, this book is for you.

Installing Flash Catalyst

You must purchase the Adobe Flash Catalyst CS5 software either as a stand-alone application or as part of Adobe Creative Suite. By default, Flash Player 10, Adobe Media Encoder CS5, Adobe AIR, and Adobe Media Player are installed along with Flash Catalyst. For system requirements and complete instructions on installing the Flash Catalyst software, see the ReadMe.pdf file on the application DVD.

Install Flash Catalyst from the Adobe Flash Catalyst CS5 application DVD onto your hard disk. You cannot run the program from the DVD. Follow the onscreen instructions. Make sure that your serial number is accessible before installing the application. You can find the serial number on the registration card or on the back of the DVD case.

Optimizing performance

Flash Catalyst CS5 requires a minimum of 1 GB of RAM; 2 GB is highly recommended. The more RAM available to Flash Catalyst, the faster the application will work for you. A 1024 x 768 minimum display, with 16-bit or greater video card, is required; a 1280 x 800 or greater display is recommended.

Checking for updates

Adobe periodically provides updates to software. You can easily obtain these updates through Adobe Updater, as long as you have an active Internet connection.

1   In Flash Catalyst CS5, choose Help > Update. The Adobe Application Manager automatically checks for updates available for your Adobe software.

2   In the Adobe Application Manager dialog box, select and download the updates you want to install. A message tells you if your application is already up to date. If the application is up to date, click Quit to close the Application Manager dialog box and return to Flash Catalyst.

● **Note:** To set your preferences for future updates, click Preferences in the dialog box. Select which applications to update automatically and how you would like to be informed when new updates are available. Click Done to accept the new settings.

Flash Player version

The lessons in this book are created to work with Flash Player 10 or higher. The applications you will develop using Flash Catalyst are deployed as SWF files (the Flash Player file format) and viewed using a browser with Flash Player 10. For information on Flash Player version penetration visit:

www.adobe.com/products/player_census/flashplayer

In Lesson 12, you will publish a project as an Adobe AIR application for deploying to the desktop. When you install and play the AIR application, you may be required to install or update your version of the Adobe AIR runtime.

Copying the lesson files

Throughout the lessons in this book, you'll be working with several interactive applications. Flash Catalyst application projects are stored within a single FXP file. Most of the lessons use additional resources such as audio, video, image, and text files. To complete the lessons in this book, you must copy these files from the *Adobe Flash Catalyst CS5 Classroom in a Book* CD (located inside the back cover of this book) to your computer.

Copy the Lessons folder (which contains folders named Lesson01, Lesson02, and so on) from the *Adobe Flash Catalyst CS5 Classroom in a Book* CD onto your computer by dragging it to your hard drive.

When you begin each lesson, you will be instructed where to navigate within the Lessons folder to find all the assets you need to complete the lesson.

If you have limited storage space on your computer, you can copy each Lesson folder individually as you need it and delete it afterward if desired. Some lessons build on preceding lessons, but even then, the assets in each lesson folder are self-contained and don't require materials from other lesson folders. You do not have to save any finished project if you don't want to or if you have limited hard disk space.

How to use these lessons

Each lesson in this book provides step-by-step instructions for creating portions of a project that illustrates essential Flash Catalyst techniques. Some lessons build on projects created in preceding lessons; others stand alone. All the lessons build on each other in terms of concepts and skills, so the best way to learn from this book is to proceed through the lessons in sequential order. Some techniques and processes are explained and described in detail only the first few times you perform them. Many of the most essential processes are repeated throughout the exercises so that you can build a familiarity as well as a level of comfort with the basic tools in the language.

Each of the lesson folders contains the files that you will use to complete the lesson. Some of the lessons also include other files and folders with media and resources needed to complete the lesson's project. Be sure to keep each folder's content together.

Standard elements in the book

▶ **Tips:** Alternative ways to perform tasks and suggestions to consider when applying the skills you are learning.

Boldface text: Words that appear in **boldface** indicate text that you must type while working through the steps in the lessons.

Italicized text: Words that appear in *italics* are either for *emphasis* or are *new vocabulary.*

Menu commands and keyboard shortcuts: Menu commands are shown with angle brackets between the menu names and commands: Menu > Command > Subcommand. Keyboard shortcuts are shown with a dash between the names of keys to indicate that you should press the keys simultaneously; for example, Ctrl-Enter means that you should press the Ctrl and Enter keys at the same time.

● **Notes:** Additional background information to expand your knowledge and advanced techniques you can explore to further develop your skills.

Windows and Mac commands and keystrokes: When the commands or keys required to complete a task are different in the Windows and Mac operating systems, the commands or keys are separated by a forward slash. The first key or command listed is for Windows and the second one is for Mac. For example: Click Open and then click Select/Choose.

Additional resources

Adobe Flash Catalyst CS5 Classroom in a Book is not meant to replace documentation that comes with the program or to be a comprehensive reference for every feature. Only the commands and options used in the lessons are explained in this book. For comprehensive information about program features and tutorials, refer to these resources:

Adobe Community Help: Community Help brings together active Adobe product users, Adobe product team members, authors, and experts to give you the most useful, relevant, and up-to-date information about Adobe products. Whether you're looking for a code sample or an answer to a problem, have a question about the software, or want to share a useful tip or recipe, you'll benefit from Community Help. Search results will show you not only content from Adobe, but also from the community.

With Adobe Community Help you can:

- Access up-to-date definitive reference content online and offline
- Find the most relevant content contributed by experts from the Adobe community, on and off Adobe.com
- Comment on, rate, and contribute to content in the Adobe community
- Download Help content directly to your desktop for offline use
- Find related content with dynamic search and navigation tools

To access Community Help: If you have any Adobe CS5 product, then you already have the Community Help application. To invoke Help, choose Help > Flash Catalyst Help. This companion application lets you search and browse Adobe and community content, plus you can comment on and rate any article just like you would in the browser. However, you can also download Adobe Help and language reference content for use offline. You can also subscribe to new content updates (which can be automatically downloaded) so that you'll always have the most up-to-date content for your Adobe product at all times. You can download the application from www.adobe.com/support/chc/index.html

Adobe content is updated based on community feedback and contributions. You can contribute in several ways: add comments to content or forums, including links to web content; publish your own content using Community Publishing; or contribute Cookbook Recipes. Find out how to contribute: www.adobe.com/community/publishing/download.html

See http://community.adobe.com/help/profile/faq.html for answers to frequently asked questions about Community Help.

Adobe Flash Catalyst Help and Support: www.adobe.com/support/Flash Catalyst is where you can find and browse Help and Support content.

Adobe TV: http://tv.adobe.com is an online video resource for expert instruction and inspiration about Adobe products, including a How To channel to get you started with your product.

Adobe Design Center: www.adobe.com/designcenter offers thoughtful articles on design and design issues, a gallery showcasing the work of top-notch designers, tutorials, and more.

Adobe Developer Connection: www.adobe.com/devnet is your source for technical articles, code samples, and how-to videos that cover Adobe developer products and technologies.

Resources for educators: www.adobe.com/education includes three free curriculums that use an integrated approach to teaching Adobe software and can be used to prepare for the Adobe Certified Associate exams.

Adobe Forums: http://forums.adobe.com lets you tap into peer-to-peer discussions, questions, and answers on Adobe products.

Adobe Marketplace & Exchange: www.adobe.com/cfusion/exchange is a central resource for finding tools, services, extensions, code samples, and more to supplement and extend your Adobe products.

Adobe Flash Catalyst CS5 product home page: www.adobe.com/products/Flash Catalyst

Adobe Labs: http://labs.adobe.com gives you access to early builds of cutting-edge technology, as well as forums where you can interact with the Adobe development teams building that technology and with other like-minded members of the community.

Adobe certification

The Adobe training and certification programs are designed to help Adobe customers improve and promote their product-proficiency skills. There are four levels of certification:

- Adobe Certified Associate (ACA)

- Adobe Certified Expert (ACE)

- Adobe Certified Instructor (ACI)

- Adobe Authorized Training Center (AATC)

The Adobe Certified Associate (ACA) credential certifies that individuals have the entry-level skills to plan, design, build, and maintain effective communications using different forms of digital media.

The Adobe Certified Expert program is a way for expert users to upgrade their credentials. You can use Adobe certification as a catalyst for getting a raise, finding a job, or promoting your expertise.

If you are an ACE-level instructor, the Adobe Certified Instructor program takes your skills to the next level and gives you access to a wide range of Adobe resources.

Adobe Authorized Training Centers offer instructor-led courses and training on Adobe products, employing only Adobe Certified Instructors. A directory of AATCs is available at http://partners.adobe.com.

For information on the Adobe Certified programs, visit www.adobe.com/support/certification/main.html.

Accelerate your workflow with
Adobe CS Live

Adobe CS Live is a set of online services that harness the connectivity of the web and integrate with Adobe Creative Suite 5 to simplify the creative review process, speed up website compatibility testing, deliver important web user intelligence and more, allowing you to focus on creating your most impactful work. CS Live services are complimentary for a limited time* and can be accessed online or from within Creative Suite 5 applications.

Adobe BrowserLab is for web designers and developers who need to preview and test their web pages on multiple browsers and operating systems. Unlike other browser compatibility solutions, BrowserLab renders screenshots virtually on demand with multiple viewing and diagnostic tools, and can be used with Dreamweaver CS5 to preview local content and different states of interactive pages. Being an online service, BrowserLab has fast development cycles, with greater flexibility for expanded browser support and updated functionality.

Adobe CS Review is for creative professionals who want a new level of efficiency in the creative review process. Unlike other services that offer online review of creative content, only CS Review lets you publish a review to the web directly from within InDesign, Photoshop, Photoshop Extended, and Illustrator and view reviewer comments back in the originating Creative Suite application.

Acrobat.com is for creative professionals who need to work with a cast of colleagues and clients in order to get a creative project from creative brief to final product. Acrobat.com is a set of online services that includes web conferencing, online file sharing and workspaces. Unlike collaborating via email and attending time consuming in-person meetings, Acrobat.com brings people to your work instead of sending files to people, so you can get the business side of the creative process done faster, together, from any location.

Adobe Story is for creative professionals, producers, and writers working on or with scripts. Story is a collaborative script development tool that turns scripts into metadata that can be used with the Adobe CS5 Production Premium tools to streamline workflows and create video assets.

SiteCatalyst NetAverages is for web and mobile professionals who want to optimize their projects for wider audiences. NetAverages provides intelligence on how users are accessing the web, which helps reduce guesswork early in the creative process. You can access aggregate user data such as browser type, operating system, mobile device profile, screen resolution and more, which can be shown over time. The data is derived from visitor activity to participating Omniture SiteCatalyst customer sites. Unlike other web intelligence solutions, NetAverages innovatively displays data using Flash, creating an engaging experience that is robust yet easy to follow.

You can access CS Live three different ways:

1 Set up access when you register your Creative Suite 5 products and get complimentary access that includes all of the features and workflow benefits of using CS Live with CS5.

2 Set up access by signing up online and get complimentary access to CS Live services for a limited time. Note, this option does not give you access to the services from within your products.

3 Desktop product trials include a 30-day trial of CS Live services.

CS Live services are complimentary for a limited time. See www.adobe.com/go/cslive for details.

1 GETTING TO KNOW ADOBE FLASH CATALYST CS5

Lesson Overview

Using Adobe Flash Catalyst CS5, you can produce beautifully designed and highly interactive content for the web or desktop without authoring any code. This lesson introduces you to some of the key features and benefits of Flash Catalyst. You will explore the basic layout of the Flash Catalyst Design workspace, open a new project file, and preview a completed project.

You'll learn how to do the following:

- Open a new Flash Catalyst project

- Set dimensions and background color

- Switch between the Design and Code workspaces

- Find your way around the Design workspace

- Show and hide workspace panels

- Zoom and pan the artboard

- Open an existing project file

- Preview a project in a browser

- Find additional help documents, demos, and tutorials online

 This lesson will take about 50 minutes to complete. Copy the Lesson01 folder into the lessons folder that you created on your hard drive for these projects (or create it now), if you haven't already done so. As you work on this lesson, you won't be preserving the start files; if you need to restore the start files, copy them from the *Adobe Flash Catalyst CS5 Classroom in a Book* CD.

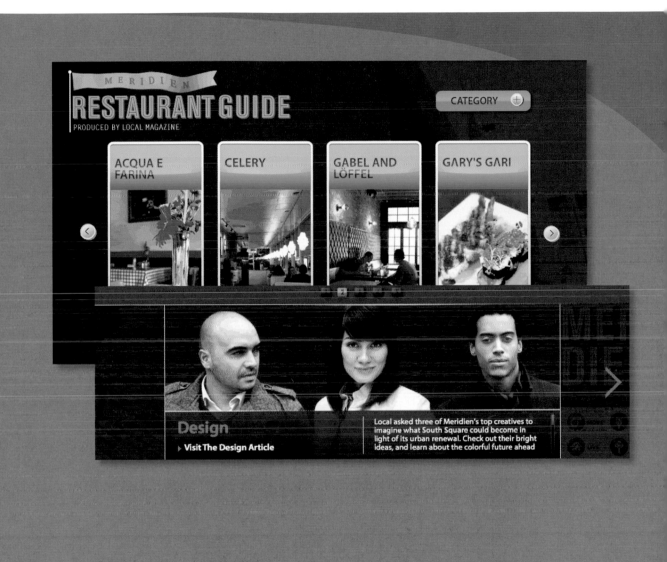

Throughout this course, you will learn the skills needed to build a wide range of rich Internet applications. Two examples used in this course include an online restaurant guide, and its companion interactive banner ad, both shown above.

About Flash Catalyst

Flash Catalyst empowers designers with complete control over the integrity of their artwork and design when producing interactive content. A common challenge for many designers is handing off static artwork and *describing* the user experience to developers. Much of their original vision is left to interpretation and sometimes lost to the limitations of data-centric development tools.

Using Flash Catalyst, designers can quickly transform their original artwork created in Adobe Photoshop, Adobe Illustrator, and Adobe Fireworks into fully functioning interactive applications, without writing a single line of code.

Is Flash Catalyst the right tool for you?

Flash Catalyst is intended for any designer who produces interactive content for the web or desktop. These designers include:

Interactive web designers and interaction designers are responsible for the visual design of interactive experiences.

Information architects create high-level interaction models for various media. Sometimes this task involves the need to quickly produce rough wireframes for the creative process.

Graphic designers and creative directors generate original artwork and interactive elements for a wide range of applications.

Rich Internet application developers work with Flash Catalyst project files to add advanced data-centric functionality.

Rich Internet applications

Whether conducting research, doing business, or purely seeking entertainment, people have come to expect a higher quality of content when surfing the web. Viewer engagement is also critical to transforming viewers into active advocates for products, brands, movements, ideas, and so on. The good news is that this has led to greater collaboration between designers and developers and to more exciting and effective content on the web. These highly interactive and engaging applications are often referred to as rich Internet applications, or RIAs.

Building RIAs with Flash Catalyst produces highly visual, interactive, and reliable cross-platform content. Adobe Flash Player reaches 98% of Internet-enabled desktops and more than 450 million devices, offering greater reach than any other client technology available. You can also use Flash Catalyst to publish Adobe AIR applications. AIR leverages the power of Flash Player while adding the capability to deploy RIAs directly to the desktop.

Key features

Flash Catalyst offers tremendous power, including some key features.

- Design using your favorite Adobe Creative Suite applications. Flash Catalyst offers a fast learning curve by leveraging what you already know in Photoshop, Illustrator, and Fireworks.

- Import and store images, video, sound, and Adobe Flash (SWF) content in the project library.

- Place objects in the exact location you want them to appear with pixel-level accuracy consistently across operating systems and devices.

- Quickly transform artwork into interactive components, such as buttons, check boxes, lists, and scroll bars.

- Create interactive forms using built-in components like text input and check boxes.

- Add interactions that define the behavior of components, such as what happens when someone clicks a button, or when predefined conditions are met.

- Add smooth animated transitions between pages or the different states (views) of a component with the click of a button.

- Round-trip edit graphics using Photoshop and Illustrator right from within the Flash Catalyst workspace.

- Create vector artwork directly in Flash Catalyst using the built-in drawing tools.

- Convert artwork into a data list that has a variable number of items or rows. The records in your data list can include images, text, or both.

- Use built-in wireframe components to create interactive prototypes.

- Publish accessible projects that are ready to deploy to the web or desktop.

Additional benefits for designers

Designers enjoy some additional benefits.

- Sell your ideas by showing functional designs rather than static screens.

- Ensure that your creative vision is accurately expressed.

- Work more efficiently when collaborating with developers to build rich Internet applications.

Flash Catalyst design workflow

There are two main types of Flash Catalyst applications. These applications include microsites and data-centric applications. You can think of a microsite as an application that is complete when published in Flash Catalyst. No additional development is required. A data-centric application requires additional development, such as integrating components with external data or web services. A Flex developer completes the development using Adobe Flash Builder. You'll learn more about data-centric applications later in this course. As when creating any project, following a consistent workflow helps in project management. The workflows for designing microsites and data-centric applications are similar. Both include these general steps.

Plan the application.

Create interface artwork — Interaction design — SWF / AIR Publish

Begin with a detailed project specification. This specification describes each page or screen, including user navigation, the artwork on each page, interactive components, and the different states of each component.

Create or acquire assets, such as artwork, video, and sound.

Create the artwork, video, and sound for the application. You can create a layered design document in Photoshop, Illustrator, or Fireworks.

Bring assets into Flash Catalyst.

Note: If you import an Illustrator file with multiple artboards, each artboard is added to a different page state in Flash Catalyst. You can also import individual Photoshop Layer Comps directly to separate page states in Flash Catalyst.

Import the design document you created in Photoshop, Illustrator, or Fireworks. Bring additional graphic files and assets, such as video, sound, and animated content published in the SWF file format. SWF files can be used to deliver static and animated vector graphics, text, video, and sound. For data-centric components, such as a data list, import a representative sample of the data (text or images).

Create and modify pages.

A Flash Catalyst project typically begins with one page state. Duplicate this page or add pages according to the project specification. Show and hide the artwork in each page state to create the different pages or screens of your application. You can also use other assets that you've imported, such as video.

Create interactive components.

Convert your original artwork to interactive components, such as buttons, scroll bars, panels, and lists. Or use Flash Catalyst wireframe components to quickly add common elements with a generic appearance. You can design custom components for behaviors that you can't capture with the built-in components. Some designers prefer to create components before adding new page states. Adding pages and creating components are interchangeable steps.

Define component states.

Components can have multiple states, such as the up, over, down, and disabled states of a button. Create or modify the different states of each interactive component, according to your project specification.

Define interactions and transitions.

Add interactions that define what happens as users interact with the application. For example, you can add interactions that transition from one page or component state to another when a user clicks a button. You can also add interactions that play animation, control video playback, or open another web page. Using the Flash Catalyst Timelines panel, you can quickly change the timing and appearance of the animated transitions between pages and component states.

Test and publish the project.

Run the application in a browser, and then publish the project as a web or desktop application. Or, save the project file (FXP) for further development in Adobe Flash Builder.

The Adobe Flash Platform

The Adobe Flash Platform includes a collection of integrated Adobe technologies for designing, creating, deploying, and viewing rich Internet applications, content, and video to the widest possible audience.

FC Adobe Flash Catalyst CS5 is an interaction design tool used to rapidly create expressive interfaces and interactive content without writing code.

FB Adobe Flash Builder is an integrated development environment (IDE) for developing cross-platform data-centric content. Developers create entire applications using Flash Builder, or import a project created using Flash Catalyst and then use Flash Builder to connect the application to data and web services.

Fx Adobe Flex is the open-source framework for both Flash Catalyst and Flash Builder.

Fl Adobe Flash Professional CS5 is an interactive multimedia content authoring environment for designers and developers who want pixel-perfect typographic fidelity and layout, more realistic animation effects, and code authoring. Content created in Flash Professional can be imported into Flash Catalyst projects as SWF files.

ƒ Adobe Flash Player is a cross-platform browser plug-in that delivers rich web experiences. Flash Player must be installed to view content created in Flash Catalyst, Flash Builder, and Flash Professional.

The Adobe AIR runtime lets developers build rich Internet applications that run on the desktop, without a browser or Internet connection. You can publish a Flash Catalyst project as an Adobe AIR application.

Adobe Flex framework and MXML

The applications you build with Flash Catalyst are Flex applications. Flex is an open-source framework for building and deploying applications that run on all major web browsers, desktops, and operating systems. MXML is the language developers use to define the layout, appearance, and behaviors in Flex applications. ActionScript 3.0 is the language used to define the client-side application logic. When you publish a Flash Catalyst project, your MXML and ActionScript are compiled as a SWF file.

Flex includes a prebuilt class library and application services. These services include data binding, drag-and-drop management, interface layout, and animation for things like smooth page transitions. The Flex component library includes interface controls such as simple buttons, check boxes, data grids, and rich text editors.

The Flex compiler is available as a stand-alone utility in the Adobe Flex 4 software development kit (SDK), or as part of the Adobe Flash Builder software. Design and development can occur in Flash Catalyst, Flash Builder, or an integrated development environment (IDE) of your choice.

Opening a new Flash Catalyst project

When you first start Flash Catalyst, you are presented with the Welcome screen.

From the Welcome screen, you can open an existing project, create a new blank project, or create a new project from a design file.

1   Start Flash Catalyst.

2   In the Create New Project section of the Welcome screen, choose Adobe Flash Catalyst Project.

The New Project dialog box opens and is where you name the project and enter values for the size and color of the artboard.

3 Enter a name for the project.

4 Set the width, height, and color, and click OK.

A new blank project opens. By default, the Design workspace is open.

▶ **Tip:** If you already have a project open, choose File > New Project to begin a new blank project.

Finding your way around

The Flash Catalyst user interface has two workspaces. These workspaces include Design and Code. Each workspace contains its own set of panels and tools.

Design workspace

The Design workspace shows a graphical representation of your application. This workspace includes the panels and tools used to create and edit projects.

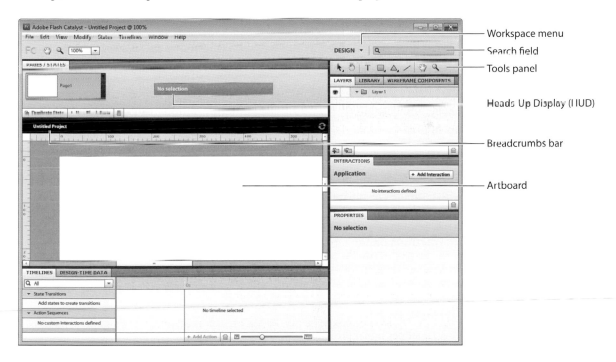

Workspace menu

Use the Workspace menu to toggle between the Design and Code workspaces.

Artboard

The artboard represents what users see when they view the published application. The artboard is where you place artwork, interactive components, and other objects that make up the application interface.

Pages/States panel

The Pages/States panel displays a thumbnail for each page in the application. If a component is selected, it shows the different states for the selected component. You can duplicate, remove, add, and rename pages and component states according to your project specification.

Tools panel

The Tools panel includes tools for creating, selecting, and transforming objects, including simple lines, shapes, and text.

Layers panel

The Layers panel is an organized collection of the objects in the application (artwork, components, video, and so on). If you import a design document created in Illustrator, Photoshop, or Fireworks, the original layer structure is preserved. As you add pages and component states to the application, you use the Layers panel to show or hide objects in each state.

Library panel

The Library panel displays the entire list of reusable assets (components, images, media, and optimized graphics) available in the project, including objects that do not appear in any page or state.

Wireframe Components panel

The Wireframe Components panel includes ready-to-use interactive components with a simple default appearance. You can drag these components to the artboard and use them "as is" or modify them to fit the appearance of your application.

Interactions panel

You can use the Interactions panel to add interactions that define what happens as users interact with the application.

Timelines panel

The Timelines panel provides controls for creating and editing transitions and action sequences. You can also use the Timelines panel to control the playback of video and SWF content, and to add sound effects.

Design-Time Data panel

After creating a Data List component, use the Design-Time Data panel to populate the list with sample design-time data. Design-time data demonstrates the appearance and behavior of the list. A developer can use Flash Builder to replace the sample design-time data with real data stored outside the application.

Properties panel

Use the Properties panel to edit the properties for selected objects, such as graphics, text, and components. The available properties change as you select different object types in the artboard, Layers panel, or Timelines panel.

Breadcrumbs bar

As you edit components, or parts within a component, Flash Catalyst keeps track of where you are in the project using breadcrumbs. You can use the Breadcrumbs bar to close an object that you are editing and return to the project artboard.

Search field

Entering a term in the Search field opens the Adobe Community Help Client and displays access to online Help and best practices.

Heads-Up Display

The Heads-Up Display (HUD) provides access to commands related to the current action or currently selected object. It appears automatically when Flash Catalyst detects that you must carry out some action. For example, the HUD appears when you select artwork on the artboard, giving you the choice of converting the artwork to a component. You can use the HUD to quickly create components.

Tip: If you don't see the HUD when you select an object, select Window > HUD, or press F7.

When converting objects to components, the HUD displays a message if further steps are required to complete the component. The instructions in the HUD message explain what you need to do next to finish creating the new component.

Code workspace

To view the Code workspace, choose Code from the Workspace menu.

The Code workspace shows the underlying MXML code. This code is generated automatically as you work in Flash Catalyst. Viewing the MXML code gives you the opportunity to understand how the application is programmed. The Code workspace contains several panels to help identify code issues.

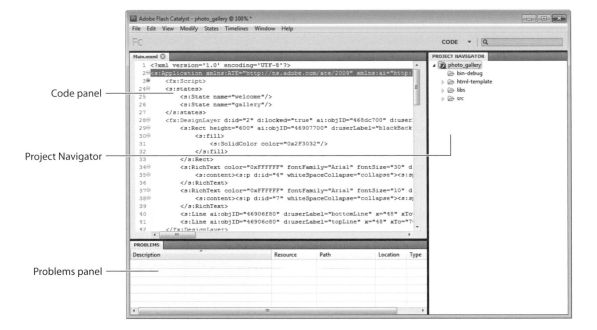

Code panel

The Code panel shows the underlying MXML code that Flash Catalyst creates automatically as you design your application. The Code workspace is read-only, which means that you can only view the code. To edit the code, open the project in Adobe Flash Builder.

Problems panel

The Problems panel shows any errors in the current MXML code. You can double-click an error in the Problems panel to locate the error in the Code panel.

Project Navigator panel

The Project Navigator panel shows the Flex project directory structure and files being created as you design your project. All of these files are wrapped within a single Flash Catalyst project file (.fxp), until you publish the project.

> ▶ **Tip:** You can also change workspaces by choosing Window > Design Workspace or Window > Code Workspace.

Opening an existing Flash Catalyst project

To help you understand the structure and layout of a typical Flash Catalyst project, here's a sample application file that includes multiple page states and various interactive components.

The example used here is an interactive restaurant guide.

1 Choose File > Open Project and browse to the Lesson01 folder from the CD.

2 Select the RIA.fxp file, and click Open.

This project includes three main page states named Start, Home, and SubPages.

● **Note:** Flash Catalyst projects have the .fxp filename extension.

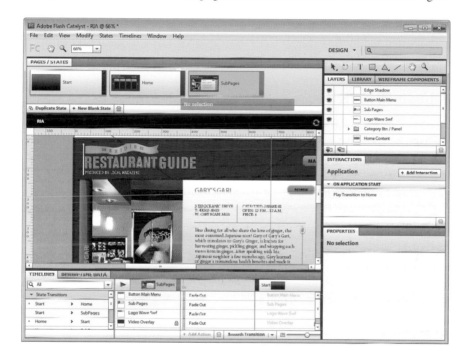

▶ **Tip:** You have a couple of other ways to open an existing Flash Catalyst project.

· You can choose Open Project in the Welcome screen.

· You can use the keyboard shortcut Ctrl+O/Command+O.

Exploring the Design workspace

As you build your application in Flash Catalyst, you'll need to navigate the Design workspace. You'll find it helpful to rearrange the workspace as you perform various tasks. For example, you may want to close or resize one panel to see more of another one. You can also view the entire artboard to get the big picture, and then quickly zoom in extremely close for precise editing.

You should still have the RIA.fxp file open.

Moving around the workspace

Most projects include more than one page. You can move from one page to another by using the Pages/States panel. Some panels share the same screen space. To use a panel, click its tab to bring it to the foreground.

1   Click the Wireframe Components panel tab to bring it to the foreground.

2   Click the Layers panel tab to bring it to the foreground.

3   In the Pages/States panel, click the picture (not the name) for the Home page.

    The contents of the Home page are shown in the artboard.

4   Click through each of the three pages in the Pages/States panel to view the various images, components, text, and video. As you move from page to page, pay attention to the Layers panel and to how the assets on each page are organized. Notice that some layers are hidden, while others are visible.

Adjusting panels

Many panels share the same location in the workspace, and sometimes a panel needs to be stretched to see more of its contents. You can resize a panel by dragging its borders. You can also double-click a panel tab to collapse or expand the entire panel or panel group.

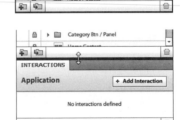

1   Click the Layers panel to select it.

    The project includes several layers, but some of these layers may not be visible.

2   Position the pointer along the gray border between the Interactions panel and the Layers panel.

    The pointer changes to a two-headed arrow.

3   Drag the border down to make more room for the Layers panel above it.

    You can also drag the border between the artboard and the panels on the right, or the Timelines and Design-Time Data panels below.

4   Double-click the Timelines panel tab.

    The Timelines and Design-Time Data panels collapse (or expand if they were already collapsed).

    Double-clicking an open panel collapses the entire panel, along with any other panels that share the same location in the workspace.

5 Double-click the Timelines panel tab again to reopen it.

6 Choose Window > Hide All Panels (or press the F4 key).

Hiding all panels is helpful when you need more space to view the artboard.

7 Choose Window > Show All Panels (F4) to unhide the panels.

8 Choose Window > Reset Workspace and click OK to return the workspace to its default settings.

Zooming the artboard

Depending on the size of your computer monitor and the dimensions of your application, you may need to zoom or pan the artboard as you work. You can use the Zoom Magnification menu, located above the artboard, to view the artboard at between 25% and 800% of actual size. You can also use the Zoom tool, located above the artboard in the Tools panel, to zoom in to a specific part of the artboard.

1 Select SubPages in the Pages/States panel.

This page includes several components and artwork. You may need to zoom in and out as you work with this page.

2 Click the arrow to the right of the Zoom Magnification field (100% ▾) to open the Zoom Magnification menu, and choose 50%.

3 Use the horizontal and vertical scroll bars beside the artboard to center the application in the workspace.

You can now see more of the artboard at one time. You are not limited to the percent settings in the Zoom Magnification menu. You can also type your own setting directly in the Zoom Magnification field.

4 Double-click 50% in the Zoom Magnification field, type **30**, and press Enter/ Return.

The artboard zooms to 30% of actual size.

5 Select the Zoom tool (🔍).

6 Position the Zoom tool over the artboard and click several times to zoom in to 800% of actual size.

Zooming in is helpful for precise editing and placement of artwork in your application.

7 Hold down the Alt/Option key, and notice the Zoom tool now has a minus sign on it (🔍). Click twice to zoom back out to 200% of actual size.

8 Choose View > Fit Artboard In Window.

The artboard adjusts to fit within the workspace window.

▶ **Tip:** You can also zoom in and out or select a zoom magnification from the View menu.

Panning the artboard

You may find it helpful to pan (move right and left) the artboard, as an alternative to scrolling. This is especially helpful when zoomed in close. You can pan the artboard using the Hand tool, which is located above the artboard and in the Tools panel.

1 Select the Hand tool (✋).

2 Using the Hand tool, drag to view a different part of the artboard.

You can also pan the artboard by moving the scroll bars, but by using the Hand tool you can do this in one step.

Previewing a project in a browser

Before publishing a project, you can run and test the application in a web browser. This is something you will do often when creating projects in Flash Catalyst.

You should still have the RIA.fxp file open.

1 Choose File > Run Project, or press Ctrl+Enter/Command+Return.

Flash Catalyst compiles the project and the project opens in your default web browser. The first page state of this project begins with a video and then presents the main navigation elements. This application includes an animated SWF movie, buttons, data lists, and several custom interactive components.

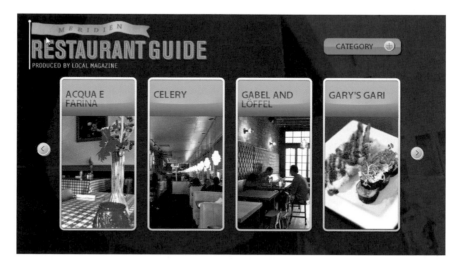

2 Explore and test the application by doing the following:

- Mouse over the interactive components to view their behavior.

- Click the right and left navigation buttons to browse additional items in the list of restaurants.

- Click any item in the list (any restaurant) to view more information.

- Click Gallery and Build Your Order.

- Click Main Menu to return to the first page of the application.

- Open and close the Category menu.

3 Choose File > Open Project.

A message prompts you to save your change. You cannot have more than one Flash Catalyst project open at the same time.

4 Click No to close the project without saving.

5 In the Open dialog box, browse to the Lesson01 folder and open the Banner.fxp file.

This is another project that you'll work on during this course. It's an interactive advertisement banner.

6 Choose File > Run Project to preview the application in a browser.

Click through each of the five pages using the numbered navigation buttons at the top of the banner.

Note: Even though this application has only three main page states, there are several different views. This was accomplished by creating custom components. By nesting components inside other components you can add to the structure and depth of the application without adding pages. You'll learn more about components later in this course.

2 WHEELS GOOD

Visit The Feature Article

What do architectural landmarks, transportation whiz kids, Friar's Market, local growers, the "Green Light" district, and Le Bon Mot have in common? They're Alexis K.'s

Getting Flash Catalyst Help

You can gain quick access to online help right from within the Flash Catalyst application workspace. Flash Catalyst Community Help is a new integrated online help environment of instruction, inspiration, and support using a custom search to get the most relevant results.

1 Choose Help > Flash Catalyst Help.

If you are prompted to install the Community Help application or the Adobe AIR application, follow the prompts to install these programs.

Your default web browser is started and you are taken to the Flash Catalyst Community Help page.

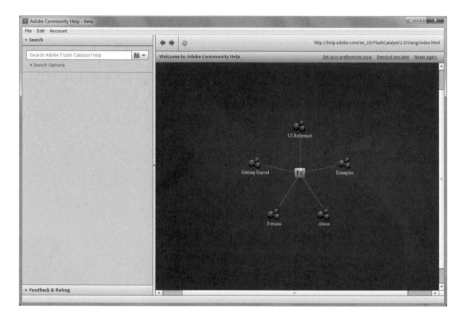

You can use the navigation links on the right to select from common help topics, such as "Getting Started," or "UI Reference." You can also use the Search field in the left pane to perform a key word search.

2 Select a topic and browse the Community Help topics.

3 Close the browser window and return to Flash Catalyst.

4 In the Flash Catalyst Design workspace, click in the Community Help Search field, type a search term or phrase, and press Enter/Return.

Your default web browser is started and you are taken to the Flash Catalyst Community Help search results. The results include links to matching content provided by Adobe and by the Flash Catalyst community at large.

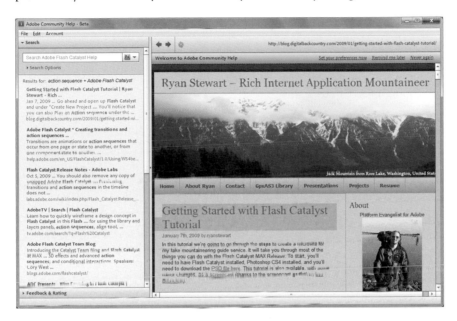

5 Close the browser window and return to Flash Catalyst.

6 Choose File > Close Project. If you are prompted to save changes, click No.

The project closes and you return to the Welcome screen.

Review questions

1 Which Adobe Creative Suite applications are used to produce layered design documents for import into a new Flash Catalyst project?

2 How does Flash Catalyst benefit designers who want to create interactive content without writing code?

3 When you first start Flash Catalyst, what are two things you can do from the Welcome screen?

4 Where in the Design workspace do you place and manipulate artwork?

5 What Flash Catalyst feature is used to organize the different screens or main areas within the application interface?

6 In addition to using the Flash Catalyst menus, which part of the Design workspace can you use to convert artwork into components?

7 What part of the Design workspace is used to show or hide artwork in a selected page or component state?

Review answers

1 You can use Adobe Photoshop, Adobe Illustrator, and Adobe Fireworks to create your layered design and artwork.

2 Flash Catalyst helps designers sell their ideas by showing functional designs rather than static screens. Flash Catalyst ensures that each design is accurately expressed, and it allows more efficient collaboration between designers and developers who build rich Internet applications.

3 From the Welcome screen, you can begin a blank Flash Catalyst project or open an existing project.

4 The artboard is where you place and work with artwork, interactive components, and other objects that make up the application interface.

5 The Pages/States panel displays a thumbnail for each page in the application. You can duplicate, remove, add, and rename pages and component states according to your project specification.

6 The Heads-Up Display (HUD) appears automatically when Flash Catalyst detects that you must carry out some action. The HUD appears when you select artwork on the artboard, giving you the choice to convert the artwork to a component.

7 The Layers panel is an organized collection of the objects in the application. As you add pages and component states to the application, you use the Layers panel to show or hide objects in each state.

2 PREPARING, IMPORTING, AND PLACING ARTWORK

Lesson Overview

It's a common complaint. You've spent hours perfecting artwork and layout—positioning images to the exact pixel, choosing a perfect stroke, tweaking fades and filters, and organizing layers to clearly show the relationship between various states of interactive objects. But still, you worry that the finished product won't look or behave the way you want. Your vision is often compromised by limitations in development tools, or simply lost in translation—but not anymore. With Flash Catalyst, you can preserve the integrity of your artwork, from vision to publishing.

In this lesson, you'll learn how to do the following:

- Prepare a design document for import

- Export an FXG file from Adobe Fireworks

- Import a layered design document into Flash Catalyst

- Select fidelity options when importing a design document

- Import artwork into Flash Catalyst

- Position artwork in the Flash Catalyst artboard

- Optimize artwork

 This lesson will take about 45 minutes to complete. Copy the Lesson02 folder into the lessons folder that you created on your hard drive for these projects (or create it now), if you haven't already done so. As you work on this lesson, you won't be preserving the start files; if you need to restore the start files, copy them from the *Adobe Flash Catalyst CS5 Classroom in a Book* CD.

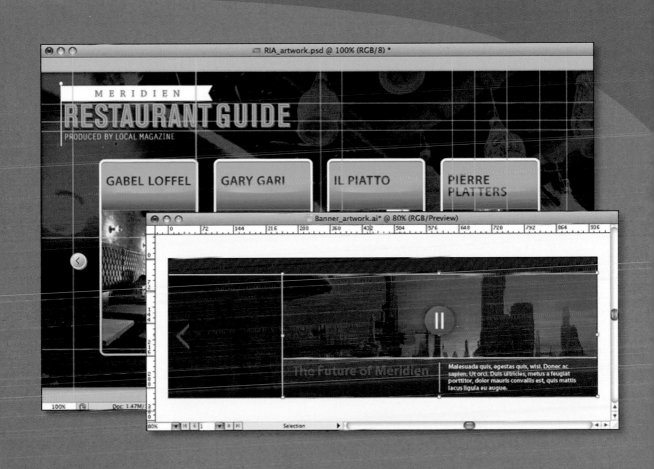

Flash Catalyst is tightly integrated with leading design tools from Adobe, including Adobe Illustrator and Adobe Photoshop. You can create and edit artwork using your favorite design tools, and then use Flash Catalyst to turn static objects into fully functioning rich Internet applications.

Preparing a design document

Knowing that you can turn your static artwork into working applications is pretty exciting. But before you get started, take a moment to review these best practices for preparing your design document. The way you approach the design and organization of your artwork has a significant impact on the structure of the project in Flash Catalyst and the underlying code. The following ideas will help protect the integrity of your design and minimize re-working or re-structuring assets after bringing them into Flash Catalyst.

Choose your design application

▶ **Tip:** When choosing Adobe Illustrator as your design application for Flash Catalyst artwork, use the Illustrator Flash Catalyst document preset. In the Create New section of the Adobe Illustrator Welcome screen, choose Create Flash Catalyst Document.

Flash Catalyst imports files saved in the Flash XML Graphics format (FXG). You can generate the FXG file from any document created in Adobe Fireworks, Adobe Illustrator, or Adobe Photoshop.

In fact, if you create your design using Photoshop or Illustrator, you can save yourself the step of exporting the FXG file. Flash Catalyst has an import feature that makes opening PSD and AI files a cinch! We'll get to that in a moment.

▶ **Tip:** In Photoshop and Fireworks, set your design document color mode to RGB. Spot and process colors are not supported in Flash Catalyst. Set an image resolution of 72 pixels per inch.

What is FXG?

When creating structured graphics for use in Adobe Flex or Adobe Flash Catalyst, you can save your design in the Flash XML Graphics format (FXG). FXG is a graphics file format based on a subset of MXML, the XML-based programming language used by the Flex framework. You can use FXG files in Adobe Flash Catalyst to develop rich Internet applications and experiences. When saving as FXG, images must be under 6,777,216 total pixels and less than 8,192 pixels in width or height.

Plan the structure of your application

There are different approaches to structuring your application. The two most common ways to structure the application are:

- Import all artwork in the design document to a single page state. Distribute artwork to pages in Flash Catalyst using the Flash Catalyst Pages/States and Layers panels.

- Define the main pages of the application in your design document using Layer Comps in Photoshop or multiple artboards in Illustrator.

In both approaches your design document includes a hierarchy of clearly named layers and groups to define the pages and functional component of the application. Any layers and groups that you define in Illustrator, Photoshop, or Fireworks are maintained when you import the project into Flash Catalyst.

Importing all artwork to a single page state

When you create a new Flash Catalyst document by importing an FXG file, Photoshop document, or Illustrator document with a single artboard, your artwork appears on one new page state in Flash Catalyst. You can then duplicate or add pages and use the Flash Catalyst Layers panel to define which artwork appears on each page. This is a common workflow for structuring your application in Flash Catalyst, and that's what we'll be doing in this course.

Using Photoshop Layer Comps and multiple Illustrator artboards

A Photoshop Layer Comp (composition) provides a snapshot of which layers are turned on and off in your Photoshop document. When preparing a document for import to Flash Catalyst, you can use Layer Comps to represent each page state in your Flash Catalyst application. You can then import each Layer Comp to a different state in Flash Catalyst. To do this, you need to import each Layer Comp separately using the advanced options in the Photoshop Import Options dialog box. When you import artwork in a Photoshop Layer Comp, the artwork is centered in the Flash Catalyst artboard. To preserve the layout and positioning of your Layer Comps, include a background layer that is the same size as the Flash Catalyst artboard.

When you import an Illustrator document with multiple artboards, each artboard appears on a separate page state in Flash Catalyst.

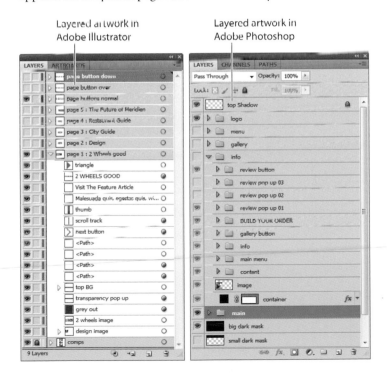

Layered artwork in Adobe Illustrator

Layered artwork in Adobe Photoshop

The organization of your content is extremely important. You'll need to identify and select these objects when separating artwork onto different pages and states or converting artwork into functional components in Flash Catalyst.

Here are some tips for organizing your artwork using layers:

- Use top-level layers (or Layer Groups in Photoshop) to represent the main pages or screens of the application.

- Add a layer for common objects that appear on every page. For example, you may want a layer named "background" or a layer named "navigation."

- Use sublayers (or layers within a Layer Group in Photoshop) to represent the elements on each page.

- Use sublayers to organize the building blocks or *parts* of individual Flash Catalyst components such as scroll bars, menus, and buttons.

Group complex objects

Much of the artwork you create is made from a collection of complex parts, including images, shapes, lines, text, symbols, and so on. Grouping complex objects before bringing them into Flash Catalyst makes them easier to manage.

Flatten artwork with filters and effects

▶ **Tip:** Flash Catalyst includes a small collection of filters, including blurs, shadows, bevels, and glows. You can apply these to objects by using the Properties panel in Flash Catalyst.

In Illustrator, Photoshop, and Fireworks, you can use layers to apply a large selection of filters and effects to artwork and text. Some examples include drop shadows, opacity masks, and blends. In Photoshop these are called *Adjustment layers*. By placing the effect or filter in a separate layer, you preserve the original artwork or text. Unfortunately, not all filters and effects import correctly into Flash Catalyst.

When you import a Photoshop file, Flash Catalyst rasterizes all Layer Effects for image, shape, and text layers. Use the following settings to help preserve the appearance of artwork created in Photoshop:

- For text layers with effects or masks, use Vector Outlines or Flatten Bitmap Image.

- For masks applied at the Layer Group level, use Flatten Bitmap Image.

- For opacity changes at the Layer Group level, use Flatten Bitmap Image.

The following Illustrator filters are supported in Flash Catalyst. All other filters and effects are rasterized or expanded during import.

- Drop Shadow

- Inner Glow

- Outer Glow

- Gaussian Blur

Name everything

The layer names you use in the original design document are brought into Flash Catalyst. These names are also reflected in the Flex code that gets generated by Flash Catalyst. This is the same code that will be used by Flex developers if the Flash Catalyst project file is imported into Flash Builder for additional development.

Use a consistent naming strategy throughout your design. For example, you could use "name_btn_up" and "name_btn_down" to specify artwork that will be turned into button components. It's a good idea to agree on a naming convention with other designers and developers before beginning a project.

Embed images in the design document

Most rich Internet application projects involve a team of designers and developers working together in an iterative process. By placing images within your design file, rather than linking to them, you can share a single file and you'll know that everyone has the assets they need to continue working on the project. Images and other assets appear in the Library panel within Flash Catalyst.

Manage fonts when sharing files

When collaborating with teams, make sure that everyone has the necessary fonts installed. This is essential if you plan to keep your text editable, for example if the design includes body copy that needs to change over time. Even with the necessary fonts installed, editable text doesn't always look the same when brought into Flash Catalyst. Things like kerning or leading may differ. For text objects that need to look exactly as you've designed them (a logo is a good example), you can:

- Convert text to a shape or bitmap (raster) image.

- Convert text to vector outlines in Illustrator.

Identify duplicate component assets

It's often necessary to include repeated buttons, text input areas, and other visual elements to represent the overall visual design of the application. In Flash Catalyst, you want to define a single object for each unique piece of artwork, but avoid defining objects where the artwork is the same. To make your work easier in Flash Catalyst, you can identify any duplicate items in your design document.

There are several ways to do this. You can use a unique naming convention for duplicate components, such as inputText (for the master) and _inputText (for a duplicate). Another option is to identify them visually using color or opacity.

Identify reusable objects, such as this text field. In Flash Catalyst, you can delete the duplicate objects and use copies (instances) of a single object.

Set component properties in Flash Catalyst

Before you begin a design, take a few minutes to explore the available properties for formatting text, shapes, and components in Flash Catalyst. This will help you determine which objects and states to define in the design document, and which to save for Flash Catalyst.

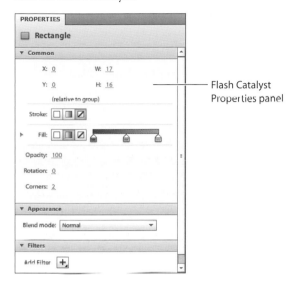

Flash Catalyst Properties panel

Create sample artwork for a list of images or text

When browsing the web, you may notice that lots of applications include scrolling lists of data (images and text). In Flash Catalyst, a Data List component is used to display a collection of data that is stored outside the application. When designing artwork for a Data List component that will be bound to an external data source, you don't need to include every item in the list, just a representative model. A best practice when preparing your design document is to include the first item and a separate group that serves as a guide for alignment and spacing.

You will use the first item in the list as the repeating part of the Data List component.

The group is used for spacing and alignment only and can be thrown away when you create the Data List component.

Hide, show, and lock layers

When you import a layered design document into Flash Catalyst, the layer structure is preserved. This includes which layers are locked or hidden. You can save yourself a few steps by locking layers that you don't need to edit, such as background or border graphics. You can also hide layers that are hidden in their initial state, such as the over and down states for an interactive button.

Exporting an FXG file from Adobe Fireworks

Adobe Fireworks users may feel a little left out when they first launch Flash Catalyst. One of the first things they'll notice is the absence of a direct Fireworks import option in the Welcome screen. In reality, Flash Catalyst imports only FXG documents regardless of where they originated—in Photoshop, Illustrator, or Fireworks. Flash Catalyst just happens to have the ability to convert your PSD and AI files into the FXG format automatically. Following are the general steps for exporting an FXG file from Fireworks to import into Flash Catalyst. The steps to export an FXG file from Fireworks CS4 and CS5 are different. Refer to the appropriate steps below for instructions on exporting FXG files from your version of Fireworks.

Fireworks CS4

1. Start Adobe Fireworks CS4 and open the design document you want to import into Flash Catalyst.

2. Choose Commands > Export To FXG.

   The Select Folder dialog box appears.

3. Locate and select a destination folder for the FXG file.

4. Enter a name for the file and click OK.

   You can now import the FXG file into Flash Catalyst.

Fireworks CS5

1. Start Adobe Fireworks CS5 and open the design document you want to import into Flash Catalyst.

2. Choose File > Export.

   The Export dialog box appears.

3. Open the Export pop-up menu and choose FXG And Images.

4. Open the Pages pop-up menu and select which pages to include in the FXG.

5. Click Save.

   You can now import the FXG file into Flash Catalyst.

Importing artwork

Fantastic! You've followed the recommended best practices. Now your design document is ready to go from static art to a living application—complete with motion graphics, animated transitions, and interactive controls.

There are four ways to get your artwork into Flash Catalyst.

- Import a layered design document created in Adobe Photoshop, Adobe Illustrator, or Adobe Fireworks. This is the preferred method for beginning a new project in Flash Catalyst.
- Import images using the File > Import > Image command in Flash Catalyst.
- Copy and paste graphics into the Flash Catalyst artboard.
- Import a Flash Catalyst library package. You will learn how to create a library package later in this course.

Import a design document

You can import a design document from the Flash Catalyst Welcome screen.

1 Start Flash Catalyst.

The Welcome screen includes three options for importing a design file: From Adobe Illustrator AI File, From Adobe Photoshop PSD File, and From FXG File. For this task, you will import an Adobe Illustrator file.

● **Note:** Flash Catalyst imports design documents that are less than 40MB.

● **Note:** When you import an FXG file exported from a multilayered Fireworks document, all objects import as a group. You can break these objects into multiple layers in Flash Catalyst by ungrouping them.

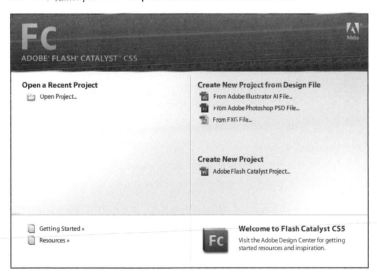

2 In the Create New Project from Design File section of the Welcome screen, choose From Adobe Illustrator AI File.

The Import dialog box appears.

3 Browse to the Lesson02 folder on your hard drive. Select the Banner_artwork.ai file and click Open.

The Illustrator Import Options dialog box appears. The artboard size and color match the document you're importing. The fidelity options include settings that determine how Flash Catalyst imports objects with filters, gradients, text, and blends. Fidelity refers to how well the imported artwork matches the original. See the "Import fidelity options" sidebar for more information on each setting.

The Import Non-Visible Layers option is selected by default. Typically, you want this selected so that every layer, including those you've temporarily hidden, are imported. Illustrator includes a built-in collection of graphics, called *symbols*. You can also create new symbols and add them to the collection. If you select Include Unused Symbols, every Illustrator symbol in the file is added to the Flash Catalyst project library. Some people think that Illustrator symbols import to Flash Catalyst as reusable components in the library. Illustrator symbols import as Optimized Graphics.

4 Click OK.

The Illustrator file is converted to the FXG format automatically and then imported directly into a new Flash Catalyst project. Flash Catalyst informs you if the document includes a large number of bitmap images, large bitmaps, or a large number of vector paths. To improve performance, you can optimize these items.

After the document imports, you should save the file.

5 Choose File > Save. Enter a name for the project in the File Name field (or accept the suggested name). Click Save.

The project is saved. Flash Catalyst project files have the .fxp filename extension. In the next task, you will import an image that was missing in the design document. You will then place that image in the artboard.

Import fidelity options

The Illustrator import fidelity options control how Flash Catalyst handles filters, gradients, text, and blends. The Photoshop import fidelity options control how Flash Catalyst imports image, shape, and text layers.

In the Fidelity Options section of the dialog box, you can open the pop-up menus and choose import fidelity options. The options in the menus are similar for Photoshop and Illustrator. They include:

Keep editable (AI & PSD): Keeps the item in an editable form, even if it might lose fidelity (lose some quality or look different from the original). For example, if you choose "Keep editable" for text, then the text will import as an actual text item in Flash Catalyst. Editable text may not look exactly the same in Flash Catalyst as it did in Photoshop or Illustrator.

Expand (AI only): Converts an object with a filter into a set of vectors or bitmaps that approximate the original appearance in Illustrator. For example, expanding a drop shadow filter on a rectangle might create an image of the drop shadow behind the original rectangle.

Flatten (AI & PSD): Converts objects into a single bitmap (raster) image.

Vector outlines (AI & PSD): Converts text into a vector path that approximates the rendered appearance of the text.

Crop (PSD Shape layers only): The vector mask that defines a shape in Photoshop Shape layers is imported as a mask into Flash Catalyst. However, instead of applying that mask to a bitmap that inherits the same dimensions as the original Photoshop file, this option crops the resulting bitmap to the boundary of the mask.

Automatic conversion (AI only): Flash Catalyst chooses whether to keep a given item editable, rasterize it, or convert it to vectors. The result is based on various heuristics such as the complexity of the item. For example, a simple blend might be expanded to vectors, whereas a complex blend (that would produce a lot of paths) would be rasterized.

Advanced (PSD only): Click the Advanced button in the Photoshop Import Options dialog box to specify exactly which layers to import. You can select and deselect layers to import, regardless of their visibility in Photoshop. You can also choose to import specific Photoshop Layer Comps, if they exist in the document. The selected layers import to the current page state in Flash Catalyst.

● **Note:** When you import an FXG file, there are no import options.

● **Note:** In Photoshop, you can also use the advanced import options to set import fidelity options for each layer separately.

Import additional images

▶ **Tip:** You're not limited to importing a single design document. You can import other layered Photoshop, Illustrator, or FXG files into an existing Flash Catalyst project by choosing File > Import, and then choosing the type of document you want to import.

● **Note:** If you import a large image, a message appears reminding you to reduce the size of the image before importing.

▶ **Tip:** You can also copy artwork in Illustrator or Fireworks and paste it directly into the Flash Catalyst artboard.

You've spent days, maybe even weeks, getting your design perfect and you've finally imported your design document into Flash Catalyst. You've started separating artwork into meaningful pages and component states, only to realize that you're missing key images that won't be available for another week. No problem. Just leave a placeholder and import those images separately. Flash Catalyst accepts bitmap images with the filename extensions: PNG, GIF, JPG, JPEG, and JPE.

Your Flash Catalyst project should still be open from the previous task.

1 In the Flash Catalyst Layers panel, select the page1:Feature layer.

   The layer highlights in light blue, indicating that it's the target layer for new content.

2 Choose File > Import > Image.

   The Import dialog box appears.

3 Browse to the Lesson02 folder on your hard drive. Select man.jpg and click Open.

   When you import a single image, it appears in the artboard and a master copy is added to the project library. In the next task, you'll position this image in the artboard.

A single imported image is added to the artboard and the project library.

4 In the Layers panel, click the small triangle to expand the page1:Feature layer.

   The image was added as a new object in the target layer.

Position images in the artboard

When you import objects to the artboard, they're placed in the artboard of the target layer. You can position objects by dragging, nudging (using the Arrow keys), or by choosing alignment commands in the Modify menu.

1   Make sure the Select tool ( ) is selected in the Tools panel.

2   Drag the image you imported to the blank white space on the right side of the artboard. The positioning doesn't need to be perfect. You'll fix that next.

    For more precise positioning, you can use the arrow keys on your keyboard to nudge the image up, down, left, or right.

    This image is supposed to be aligned in the bottom-right corner of the artboard. To do this, you can use the Align commands in the Modify menu.

3   Make sure the image is still selected. Choose Modify > Align > Right. Then, choose Modify > Align > Bottom.

    The image is now perfectly aligned in the bottom right corner of the artboard.

Optimizing artwork

In Flash Catalyst, graphic optimization options include converting vector graphics to bitmaps, compressing images, and converting embedded images to linked files. When you import a design document, you can choose fidelity options that do some of the graphic optimization for you. But even after importing graphics into your Flash Catalyst project, you can use the optimization options in the Heads-Up Display (HUD) or the Modify menu to apply settings to individual images.

When you select artwork, the optimization options appear in the HUD. The options include:

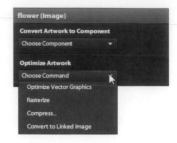

▶ **Tip:** When you select an optimized vector graphic, the Optimize Vector Graphics option changes to Break Apart Graphic. To edit the parts of a complex vector graphic that has been optimized, you must first break it apart.

Optimize Vector Graphics compiles a selected graphic into a low-level Flash object that displays more quickly in Flash Catalyst and at runtime. Once you optimize a vector drawing in Flash Catalyst, you can no longer edit its stroke and fill. In an optimized vector graphic file, all MXML information (vector, stroke, path, fill, and so on) is kept separately in an FXG file. When you optimize a vector graphic, a new optimized graphic is added to the Library panel in the Optimized Graphics category. The new optimized graphic replaces your original graphic in the artboard.

Rasterize converts a static vector graphic or text into a bitmap image. It replaces the image in the artboard with a PNG file and places a copy of the PNG in the Library panel. Use this option to optimize static vector graphics or text.

Compress adds compression to a bitmap image. It places a smaller (lower-quality) copy of the bitmap image in the Library panel. When you compress an image with transparency, the transparency is lost.

Convert To Linked Image converts an embedded image to a linked image. By default the images you add to your application are embedded and will be published as part of the SWF file. To reduce the size of your application, you can link images. Linking an image stores it outside the SWF file and loads the image when you run the application.

Optimize artwork

When you imported the Illustrator file, Flash Catalyst suggested you optimize graphics to improve the performance of your application. The gray border at the top of the artboard is made up of a rectangle shape and several small paths used to create the horizontal stripes. You don't need to work with these items separately, so you can optimize the Top Graphic.

1 In the Layers panel, click the small triangle to expand the Top Graphic layer.

   The Top Graphic layer includes two objects: Group and Rectangle.

2 Click the small triangle to expand the Group row.

   Every stripe in the graphic is a separate path.

3 Click the small triangle again to collapse the Group row.

4 In the Layers panel, click the Top Graphic layer to select all its contents.

5 In the Optimize Artwork section of the HUD, choose Optimize Vector Graphics.

The parts of the Top Graphic are combined into a single optimized graphic named Graphic1.

6 Save your changes, and then choose File > Close Project.

The project closes and you return to the Flash Catalyst Welcome screen.

Bitmap and vector graphics: What's the difference?

Flash Catalyst supports both vector and bitmap graphics, making it a very powerful design tool. For example, the artwork you import may include both vector and bitmap graphics.

Vector graphics are mathematical equations describing the distance and angle between two points. Additional information, such as the color and thickness of a line (stroke) and the contents of a path (fill) can also be set. Vectors can be sized up or down without losing image quality.

Bitmap (raster) images are made of a specific number of pixels mapped to a grid. Each pixel has a specific location and color value. An image with more pixels has a higher resolution and a larger file size.

Another example of the difference between vector and bitmap is that a photograph can accurately depict a physical scene in a single image layer. To produce similar realism in a vector illustration could require hundreds of vector shapes stacked upon each other.

This is not to suggest that bitmaps are better than vectors, or vice versa; both of these main graphic types are integral to visual communication and designing in Flash Catalyst.

The illustrations at right are examples of vector and bitmap graphics. On the left is an image created with many paths. The image on the right is a bitmap photograph.

Review questions

1 When creating a new project from a layered design document, which file types will Flash Catalyst import?

2 How does importing a layered design document created in Adobe Photoshop differ from importing a document created in Adobe Fireworks?

3 Why would you consider flattening layers before opening a design document in Flash Catalyst?

4 What can you do if you don't want text in your design document to be editable in Flash Catalyst, or if you want to ensure the text looks exactly as designed?

5 What does the Filter: Expand fidelity option do when opening an Adobe Illustrator document in Flash Catalyst?

6 What happens when you import a range of bitmap images (File > Import > Image) versus importing a single image?

7 Which type of graphic can be sized up or down without losing image quality?

Review answers

1   You can create a new Flash Catalyst project by importing Adobe Photoshop (PSD), Adobe Illustrator (AI), or FXG files.

2   You must first export an FXG file from Fireworks before the design can be opened in Flash Catalyst. There is no direct import option for layered Fireworks PNG documents. However, you can import a Photoshop document (PSD) directly from the Flash Catalyst Welcome screen, or by choosing File > Import > Adobe Photoshop File.

3   Some filters and effects are not supported in Flash Catalyst. One solution is to flatten or rasterize these objects before bringing them into Flash Catalyst.

4   If you create vector outlines or rasterize text in the original design document, it will not be editable in Flash Catalyst. You can also choose the Vector Outlines or Flatten fidelity options when importing the document in Flash Catalyst.

5   The Filter: Expand fidelity option converts an object that has a filter applied to it into a set of vectors or bitmaps that approximate the original appearance in Illustrator. For example, expanding a drop shadow filter on a rectangle might create an image of the drop shadow behind the original rectangle.

6   When you import a range of bitmap images, the images appear in the project library, but are not placed in the artboard. When you import a single image, it's placed in the library and an instance of that image is added to the target layer in the artboard.

7   Vectors can be sized up or down without losing image quality.

3 MANAGING THE LIBRARY

Lesson Overview

The Flash Catalyst project library is a storage area for the reusable content that you add to a Flash Catalyst project. This content includes the bitmap images and other media (video, sound, Adobe Flash movies, and more) that you import. You can import assets individually, as a group, or as a library package. The library also stores the components that you create—things like navigation buttons, scrolling panels, and lists of data.

In this lesson, you'll learn how to do the following:

- Identify project assets in the Library panel

- Preview images, video, and sound

- Rename assets

- Delete assets from the project

- Use and swap assets in the library

- Compress all instances of a bitmap image

- View the source of library files in the Code workspace

- Import and export a library package

 This lesson will take about 40 minutes to complete. Copy the Lesson03 folder into the lessons folder that you created on your hard drive for these projects (or create it now), if you haven't already done so. As you work on this lesson, you won't be preserving the start files; if you need to restore the start files, copy them from the *Adobe Flash Catalyst CS5 Classroom in a Book* CD.

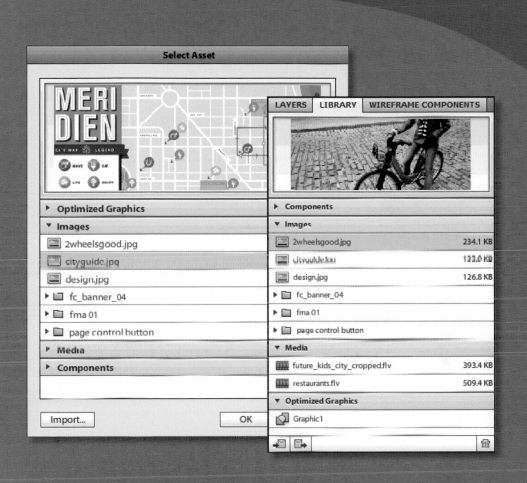

You can use the Flash Catalyst Library panel to store, locate, manage, and apply reusable components, images, Flash movies, videos, and sounds. Quickly apply global changes across your entire application. Swap images with a single click. Share your entire collection of project assets with other designers and Flex developers by using Flash Catalyst Library Packages.

Viewing the Library panel

The reusable assets that you add to a project are organized into one of four groups in the Library panel.

Images are bitmap (raster) files (PNG, GIF, JPG, JPE, JPEG) and SWF content.

Media refers to video and sound files (FLV/F4V files, mp3).

Components are the building blocks of your project. Examples of components include buttons, scroll bars, sliders, check boxes, panels, and scrolling lists.

Optimized graphics are added to the Library panel when you choose Optimize Vector Graphics in the Heads-Up Display (HUD). This is true when you optimize an image that you've imported and when you optimize an object that you've drawn using the Flash Catalyst drawing tools.

How do assets get into the Library panel?

Assets get into the Library panel in the following ways:

- When you import a design document, the bitmap images in the document are grouped together in a folder within the Images category of the Library panel. If the design document includes Illustrator symbols, the symbols are converted to optimized graphics and stored in the Optimized Graphics category.

- When you import or copy and paste a single bitmap image, SWF file, or video file, the file is added to the artboard and to the Library panel.

- When you import multiple assets at the same time, the assets are added to the Library panel, but not the artboard.

- When you import a sound file, it's added to the Library panel.

- When you import a Flash Catalyst Library Package (FXPL) that was exported from another project, the entire collection of assets is added to the Library panel.

- When you optimize an image in the artboard, an optimized copy of the image is added to the Library panel.

- If you compress an image in the Library panel or in the artboard, a compressed copy of the image is added to the Library panel.

- When you convert vector drawings into a component, optimized graphic, raster image, or compressed image, an object is added to the Library panel.

- If you add a wireframe component to the artboard and then modify it, the modified component is added to the Library panel.

Add assets to the Library panel

In this exercise, you will add a few more assets to the Library panel. When you import a single bitmap image, it's added to the artboard and the Library panel. But when you import a series of bitmaps or media files (sound and video), they're added directly to the Library panel, but not the artboard.

1   Start Flash Catalyst.

2   In the Welcome screen, choose Open Project. Browse to the Lesson03 folder on your hard drive, select the Lesson03_Banner.fxp file, and click Open.

    This is a copy of the file you created in Lesson 2, "Preparing, Importing, and Placing Artwork." It includes the images you imported from Adobe Illustrator and a single bitmap image you imported separately.

3   Select the Library panel to bring it into view.

    Library assets are divided into categories, such as Components, Images, Media, and Optimized Graphics. These categories can be expanded or collapsed by clicking the small triangle to the left of the category name.

    The Images category includes bitmap images that were imported to the project. This includes images that were imported individually or as part of a design document (AI, PSD, FXG). This also includes Adobe Flash movies (SWF files), if there are any.

    When you import a design document, its images are grouped together in a subfolder. The folder inherits the name of the original design document, which in this case is the Banner_artwork (Adobe Illustrator) document you imported in Lesson 2.

4   Expand the Banner_artwork folder.

5   Collapse the Banner_artwork folder.

6   Choose File > Import > Video/Sound File.

7   Browse to the Lesson03 folder, Shift-click to select the interlude.mp3 and restaurants.flv files, and click Open.

    The sound and video files are added to the Media category in the Library panel. This project now includes three types of assets: Images, Media, and Optimized graphics.

● **Note:** At first, the Library panel only displays categories for the types of assets that exist in the project. For example, if your project has no media, the Media category does not exist. After adding media, such as a video file, the Media category appears. Once added, the category remains in the Library panel, even after deleting all its contents.

8 Choose File > Import > Image.

9 Browse to the Lesson03 folder, Shift-click to select the 2wheels.jpg, design.jpg, future.jpg, map.jpg, and restaurants.jpg files. Click Open.

The images are added to the Library panel, but not the artboard.

10 Click to select the picture of the man in the lower-right corner of the artboard (you may need to scroll).

This was the single bitmap image that you imported in Lesson 2. In the Common category of the Properties panel, notice that the source of this image is man.jpg. There is a direct link between instances in the artboard and the source assets in the library.

The Properties panel includes a link to the source asset in the Library panel.

11 In the HUD, open the Optimize Artwork menu, and choose Optimize Vector Graphics.

● **Note:** Vector shapes that you draw in Flash Catalyst or import from Adobe Illustrator are not added to the Library panel until you convert this artwork to an optimized graphic, raster image, compressed file, or component.

The source in the Properties panel (below) changes to Graphic2.

In the Library panel (shown at right), the new optimized version of this image appears in the Optimized Graphics category.

Preview files in the Library panel

As your project grows, it can be hard to identify assets by name alone. You'll want to preview files before adding them to your application. An easy way to do this is to view the file in the preview area at the top of the Library panel.

1 Select future.jpg in the Images category of the Library panel.

   A preview of the image appears at the top of the Library panel.

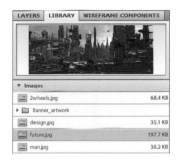

► **Tip:** When previewing interactive components in the Library panel, you only see a preview of the initial component state. To preview a component's behavior, you need to add it to the application and then run the project in a browser or publish the application.

2 In the Media category, select interlude.mp3 (a sound file) and click the Play button at the top of the Library panel.

► **Tip:** You cannot preview SWF files in the Library panel. To view a SWF animation, you must add it to the application and run the project in a browser or publish the application.

Play button   Rewind and Pause buttons

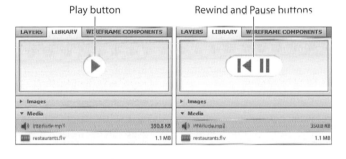

As the audio file plays, the Play button changes to the Rewind and Pause buttons.

3 In the Media category, select restaurants.flv (a video file) and click the small Play button in the lower-right corner of the preview area.

Play button   Rewind and Pause buttons

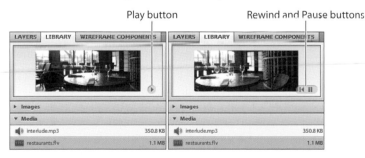

As the video plays, the Play button changes to the Rewind and Pause buttons.

4 Change to the Code workspace.

5 In the Project Navigator panel, expand the main project folder, Lesson03_Banner. Expand the src and assets folders. Expand the graphics, images, and media folders.

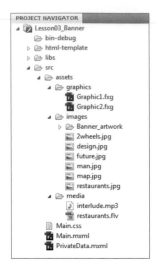

These folders store the files represented in the Library panel. For each optimized graphic, all MXML information (vector, stroke, path, fill, and so on) is kept separately in an FXG file. Project components, if there are any, are stored in an src/components directory.

6 Change back to the Design workspace.

Deleting assets from the project

Every project entails a little trial and error. As your project evolves, you'll end up with assets in the library that you no longer need in the finished application.

Eliminating outdated or unused assets from the library reduces the size of the project file, and makes the entire project more manageable. Removing unwanted assets is easy. Just delete them in the Library panel.

1 In the Images category of the Library panel, select man.jpg.

2 Click the Delete icon (🗑) in the bottom-right corner of the Library panel.

A message informs you that you can't delete the image because it's being used by the optimized graphic called Graphic2. You cannot delete an optimized graphic's source file. However, you can delete the optimized graphic or compressed copy of the image.

3 Click OK to close the message.

Note: When you delete an asset from the Library panel, it removes every instance of that asset from the project. This includes hidden pages and component states.

4 In the Optimized Graphics category, select Graphic2 and click the Delete icon (🗑).

A message informs you that removing this asset will remove the asset and all references to it. Deleting an object in the Library panel is a fast way to remove every instance of an object from the application.

5 Choose OK to delete every instance of the image.

The image vanishes from the Library panel, and from the artboard. Deleting the image left a hole in the artboard, but you'll fix that in a minute.

Compressing images in the Library panel

One of the advantages of a project library is that you can use the same assets throughout your application, and then make global changes to the project by modifying the source file in the library.

For example, you can quickly compress all instances of a bitmap (raster) image to reduce the overall file size of your application.

1 In the Images category of the Library panel, right-click man.jpg and choose Compression Options.

The Compress Image dialog box appears.

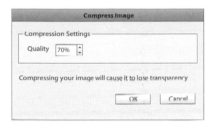

2 Leave the Quality setting at 70% and click OK.

A compressed copy of the image named man1.jpg is added to the Images category. You can tell by the reduced file size that the image is compressed.

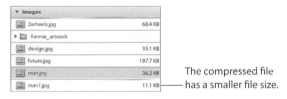
The compressed file has a smaller file size.

Renaming project assets

Just imagine if everyone you worked with were named Bob. Things could get a little confusing around the office. I suppose you could start calling people Bob1, Bob2, and so on. But that's not much better. If you're not careful, your Flash Catalyst project can end up looking like a room full of Bobs. In the world of Flash Catalyst,

▶ **Tip:** You cannot delete library assets by pressing the Delete key. However, pressing Delete removes objects that are selected in the artboard. If you have an object selected and you accidentally press the Delete key, you will remove the selected object from the current state only.

▶ **Tip:** Avoid compressing images that have transparency, because your transparency will be lost.

it's Graphic1, Graphic2, Graphic3, and so on. An easy way to avoid this is to assign descriptive names to project assets in the Library panel.

1 In the Images category of the Library panel, right-click the man1.jpg (the compressed copy of the image) and choose Rename.

   The image name is highlighted.

2 Type **man_compressed**, and press Enter/Return.

   The file is renamed in the Library panel. When you rename a file, any links to the file are updated automatically.

Using assets in the Library panel

▶ **Tip:** When you drag a library item to the artboard, a new layer is created (in the target layer folder). Best practice is to give a descriptive name to each object in the Layers panel. Renaming an instance of an item in the Layers panel does not affect the original item definition name in the Library panel.

After adding assets to the project library, you can use them over and over in different parts of your application. You simply drag the item from the Library panel and position it in the artboard.

After placing an item in the artboard, the Properties panel shows a link to the source file in the project library. You can quickly swap an object in your application with a different asset through the source link in the Properties panel.

Let's give it a try by placing the original man.jpg file in the artboard, and then swapping it for the compressed version of the same image.

1 In the Images category of the Library panel, drag man.jpg from the Library panel to the artboard.

2 Position the image in the lower-right corner of the artboard.

3 With the image still selected in the artboard, look in the Common category of the Properties panel.

   The source of this image is the man.jpg file in the Library panel. The image in the artboard is an instance of this asset and is linked to the source file in the Library panel.

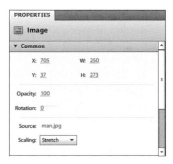

4 Click the source link, man.jpg, in the Properties panel.

The Select Asset dialog box opens with a list of assets in the Library panel. You can replace this image with another image in the library. You can also use the Import button to replace the object with a new image that you import now.

Note: If you copy and paste a bitmap, the image is added in the Layers panel and a new asset is placed in the project library. If you copy and paste a vector graphic into the artboard, a new object is added to the Layers panel but not the Library panel. That's because vector drawings are not stored in the library until you optimize them or convert them to a component.

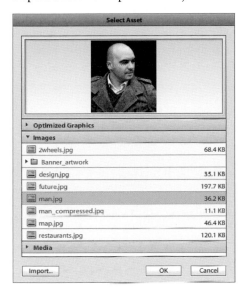

In the Images category of the Select Asset dialog box, select man_compressed.jpg and click OK.

You have just replaced the image with the smaller, compressed copy of the same picture, as indicated in the Properties panel.

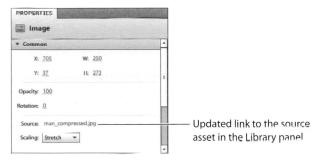

Updated link to the source asset in the Library panel

5 Choose File > Close Project, and click No when prompted to save the file.

Sharing project libraries

If you create multiple projects that leverage the same assets, or you collaborate with other designers and developers, you'll be happy to know that you can quickly share the entire contents of a Flash Catalyst project library.

Exporting a library package creates a single file containing every library item in the project. The package is saved as a Flash Catalyst Library Package (FXPL) file.

Export a library package

1   In the Welcome screen, choose Open Project. In the Lesson03 folder on your hard drive, select the Banner_completed.fxp file and click Open.

This opens a copy of the completed Banner project.

2   Open the Library panel and view the assets for this project.

The project includes over 90 assets. To recreate these in another project would be a huge task. But exporting the entire library is easy.

▶ **Tip:** Before export-ing a library package, clean up the project library by deleting any unwanted assets and giving unique and descriptive names to all assets in the library.

3   Click the Export Library Package icon at the bottom of the Library panel.

Import Library Package icon   Export Library Package icon

The Export Library Package dialog box appears. Flash Catalyst Library Package files use the .fxpl filename extension. By default, the library package uses the same name as the project from which it's exported.

4   If necessary, browse to the Lesson03 folder on your hard drive and click Save.

The entire project library is exported and stored in a file named Banner_completed.fxpl.

5   Close the project without saving changes.

Linked vs. embedded images

By default, the images you add in Flash Catalyst are embedded in the SWF file when you publish the application. You can also tell Flash Catalyst to store images outside the published application and establish a link to these files. The images are loaded by the application at runtime. Linking to large images is one way to reduce the size of the published application. It can also make updating or replacing images easier without needing to republish the application.

To convert an image from embedded to linked, right-click the image in the Library panel and choose Convert to Linked Image. The Linked Image icon appears, to show which images are linked.

Linked Image icon

▼ Images		
2wheelsgood.jpg		234.1 KB
cityguide.jpg		133.9 KB
design.jpg		126.8 KB

To embed a linked image, right-click the image in the Library panel and choose Embed Image.

Import a library package

1   In the Welcome screen, choose Adobe Flash Catalyst Project to create a new project.

The New Project dialog box appears. Normally you would match the project dimensions to the artwork, but for now just accept the default project settings.

2   Click OK to accept the default settings and open a new blank project.

A new project opens. Notice the Library panel is empty.

3   Click the Import Library Package icon.

4   In the Import Library Project dialog box, select the Banner_completed.fxpl file you created in the last task, and choose Open.

The entire library package is added to the project. The assets appear in the Library panel.

▶ **Tip:** A Flash Catalyst Library Package (FXPL) can be imported by a developer into Adobe Flash Builder as a Flex library project. These objects will maintain any behaviors, transitions, and so on, that you've added to them in Flash Catalyst.

▶ **Tip:** You can also choose File > Import > Library Package to open the Import Library Project dialog box.

● **Note:** When you add a library package to a project with existing library assets, the new assets are added to the existing library. No files are deleted.

Review questions

1 What types of assets appear in the Library panel?

2 How does a vector drawing that you create in Flash Catalyst end up in the Library panel as a reusable asset?

3 What are some different ways that you can add files to the Library panel?

4 When you select an image in the artboard, how can you tell which asset the image refers to in the Library panel?

5 What types of assets can you preview in the Library panel (list at least three)?

6 What happens to images in the application if you delete an image in the Library panel?

7 Why would you choose to include a linked image in your project?

Review answers

1 Assets in the Library panel include bitmap (raster) images, optimized graphics, components that you create from artwork, wireframe components that have been modified, SWF files, and media (video and sound).

2 You must convert a vector drawing into a component or optimized graphic before it becomes a reusable asset in the Library panel. To optimize the drawing, select it in the artboard. Then, in the HUD, open the Optimize Artwork menu and choose Optimize Vector Graphics, Rasterize, or Compress.

3 To add files to the Library panel, you can import bitmaps, SWF files, video, and sound. You can also create components and optimize artwork. Wireframe components must be modified before they appear in the Library panel.

4 The Common category in the Properties panel shows the source asset for the selected image. You can use this link to swap the image for another image.

5 You can preview images, video, sound, and components in the Library panel. However, to see the behavior of a component or SWF file, you must run the application in a browser.

6 When you delete an image from the Library panel, all instances of the image, along with any references to the image, are removed from the application.

7 Linked images are stored outside the published SWF file. Linking to large image files can reduce the published file size of the application. Linking to images allows you to update the images later without republishing the application.

4 MANAGING LAYERS

Lesson Overview

The Flash Catalyst Layers panel is like a master control center for designing your application. It provides an organized structure for viewing and managing every object in the artboard. With the click of a button, you direct which of those objects are present and visible in the current page or component state.

In this lesson, you'll learn how to do the following:

- Identify target and selected layers

- Expand and collapse layers

- Show and hide objects in the current page or state

- Lock and unlock layers, groups, and objects

- Group complex object parts

- Optimize complex groups

- Add and delete layers

- Rename objects in the Layers panel

- Use layers to locate selected objects

- Change the stacking order of objects

 This lesson will take about 30 minutes to complete. Copy the Lesson04 folder into the lessons folder that you created on your hard drive for these projects (or create it now), if you haven't already done so. As you work on this lesson, you won't be preserving the start files; if you need to restore the start files, copy them from the *Adobe Flash Catalyst CS5 Classroom in a Book* CD.

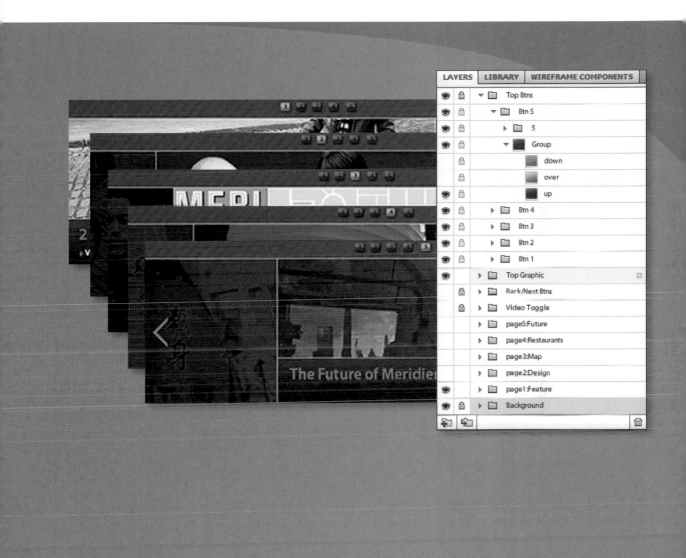

Layers are probably the most important workflow and design tools you have in Flash Catalyst. Using the Layers panel, you have complete control over every object in every state, including visibility and stacking order.

Exploring the Layers panel

Tip: A collection of related objects can be grouped in Flash Catalyst or in the design document (AI, PSD, or FXG) before importing.

The Layers panel shows every object in the application using a collection of stacked rows. Rows can represent layers, sublayers, objects (images, text, components, and so on), and groups (grouped objects). The target layer is always shaded light blue. Any objects that you add to the artboard are placed in the target layer. To select a target layer, just click in its row. A layer must be unlocked and visible to act as the target layer.

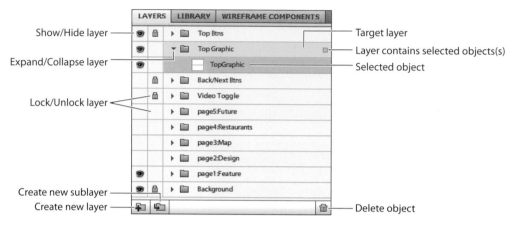

Show/Hide layer

Expand/Collapse layer

Lock/Unlock layer

Create new sublayer

Create new layer

Target layer

Layer contains selected objects(s)

Selected object

Delete object

● **Note:** Layers and sublayers are sometimes referred to as layer folders, because they are identified by a small file folder icon.

Expand and collapse layers

The Layers panel lets you organize your project using a hierarchy of related objects. Items are nested together into collapsible layers and groups for quick access and easy viewing.

1 Start Flash Catalyst. Browse to the Lesson04 folder and open Lesson04_Banner.fxp.

2 Click the Layers panel tab to bring it to the foreground.

This project includes artwork that was imported from an Adobe Illustrator file with a single artboard. The original layer structure is preserved in Flash Catalyst.

The application has ten top-level layers (layer folders), and each layer includes several objects. This project began with one new page state. Right now, all the artwork for this application is stacked together in one page state. Eventually, you will create additional pages, and then use the Layers panel to show and hide different objects in each page state. For now, let's take a closer look at the Layers panel.

3 Click the small gray triangle beside the page1:Feature layer to expand it. This is a toggle button used to expand and collapse a layer.

The page1:Feature layer holds the artwork for Page1 of the interactive banner application. It includes several objects, including one group and one sublayer.

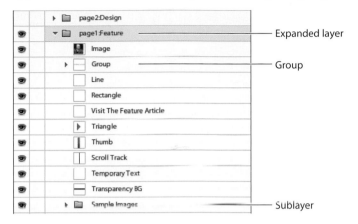

● **Note:** Layer names, such as page1:Feature, were preserved from the original design document. You can change layer names to anything you want, as long as they clearly describe their contents.

4 Collapse the page1:Feature layer.

Show and hide layers

You control which objects appear in each page or component state by selecting a state in the Pages/States panel, and then turning on and off layers. When you first add objects to a page or component state, they are present, which means they exist in that state. When an object is present, it can be made visible or hidden using the Layers panel. The following information will help to identify the presence and visibility of objects in the current state using the Layers panel:

- **Present and visible:** The name of the object is listed using dark text (present), and the eyeball icon is dark (visible).

- **Present and hidden:** The name of the object is listed using dark text (present), but there is no eyeball icon showing (hidden). If the eyeball appears dimmed, the object's visibility is on but its parent layer is hidden. When a parent layer or group is hidden, its children are hidden automatically.

- **Not present:** The name of the object is listed using dimmed text (not present). The object is not present in the current state, but it does exist in one or more other states of the application.

Try expanding and hiding the page2:Design layer.

1　Expand the page2:Design layer.

You can tell that its contents are hidden because there is no eyeball icon beside the layer name. But notice that the eyeballs for each of its objects are dimmed. A dimmed eyeball means the object is turned on, but its parent layer is currently hidden.

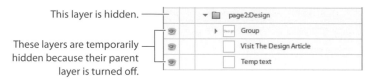

This layer is hidden. ——

These layers are temporarily — hidden because their parent layer is turned off.

2　Take a look at the artboard.

Even though we have the artwork for Page2 stacked above the artwork for Page1, we don't see it because its layer is turned off.

3　Click the empty Show/Hide box beside the page2:Design layer in the Layers panel.

The artwork for Page2 becomes visible in the artboard and the eyeball icon appears beside the layer name.

4　Click the eyeball icon beside the page2:Design layer to hide it.

Once again, the artwork for Page2 is hidden and you see the artwork for Page1. That's what you want because you're still working on Page1, as shown in the Pages/States panel.

5　Collapse the page2:Design layer in the Layers panel.

Lock and unlock layers

With so much artwork stacked in the same space, it's easy to accidentally select and move objects unintentionally. One way to protect your design is to lock objects when you're not editing them. A padlock icon indicates when an object is locked.

1 Click the Top Graphic layer to select it.

The Top Graphic (horizontal gray bar) is selected in the artboard and in the Layers panel. Clicking an object, layer, or group in the Layers panel selects all of its contents in the artboard, as long as the objects are unlocked.

2 Click the Top Btns layer.

Nothing happens because the Top Btns layer is locked, as indicated by its padlock icon.

3 Click the padlock icon beside the Top Btns layer to unlock it.

4 Click the Top Btns layer again.

This time the layer is selected, along with all of its content in the artboard. If you look in the artboard, you see that you've selected the artwork for all five navigation buttons, with a single click. Clicking layers and groups is a quick way to select multiple related objects.

5 Click the empty lock box beside the Top Btns layer in the Layers panel to lock it.

The padlock icon returns and the objects in the artboard are deselected automatically. Locked objects cannot be selected or moved.

6 In the artboard, click any of the five numbered navigation buttons.

The button you clicked is not selected, but the artwork directly below it (the Top Graphic) is. This is because the Top Btns layer is locked. Flash Catalyst selects the top-most unlocked and visible object.

Grouping objects

Groups are created in the Layers panel automatically when you group objects in the original design document. This makes their parts more manageable in Flash Catalyst. You can also group related objects after importing them. This is helpful when your design includes a large collection of parts that make up a single graphic. For example a vector drawing may include hundreds of smaller paths. Grouping them makes them a lot easier to manage in the Layers panel.

1 Expand the page1:Feature layer.

2 In the Layers panel, click to select the Line object.

▶ **Tip:** You can also Control-click/ Command-click to select a non-contiguous range of objects in the Layers panel.

3 Hold down the Shift key and click to select Transparency BG (seven rows below).

A range of eight objects is selected in the artboard and in the Layers panel.

● **Note:** Groups can be expanded in the Layers panel and ungrouped by choosing Modify > Ungroup.

4 Choose Modify > Group.

The selected objects are combined into a single Group.

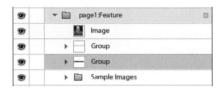

Renaming objects in the Layers panel

● **Note:** When you import artwork from a design document created in Adobe Illustrator, Adobe Photoshop, or Adobe Fireworks, the objects in the Layers panel are named automatically using the original layer names you provided in the design document.

Now that you've grouped a range of artwork in the page1:Feature layer, there are two groups with the same name. That's because all new groups are created with the default name, Group. This is also true when you add new images or components. Each new object in the Layers panel begins with a generic name, such as Image, Button, Scroll Panel, and so on. This can be a little confusing unless you take the time to assign more descriptive names.

1 In the Layers panel, double-click the Group name you created in the previous exercise.

The name is highlighted in the Layers panel.

2 Type **Panel Artwork** and press Enter/Return.

The group is renamed.

3 Collapse the page1:Feature layer.

● **Note:** The names you assign to layer folders, groups, and individual objects in the Layers panel are used for organizational purposes only. Changing names in the Layers panel does not affect the names of assets in the Library panel, and vice versa.

Optimizing complex groups

It's not uncommon for the vector artwork you import into Flash Catalyst to include complex graphics that are made up of many intricate pieces. For example, an illustration may include hundreds of individual paths that are grouped to form a single image. In addition, any text that was turned into vector outlines will import with a separate path for each individual character. If you don't need to manipulate each of these smaller parts, you can turn them into a single graphic object using the Flash Catalyst optimization options. Optimizing complex groups of artwork also makes them easier to manage in the Layers panel.

1 In the artboard (not in the Layers panel), click the large orange text that reads *2 WHEELS GOOD*.

In the artboard, it appears that you have a single object selected. If you look in the Layers panel, you see a small blue square in the page1:Feature layer. A small blue square means the row includes a selected object. This is useful for finding selected items in the Layers panel when not all layers are expanded. You can follow the blue boxes as you drill down to find the selected item(s).

2 Expand the page1:Feature layer.

You can tell by the dark blue shading that the Group row is selected.

3 Expand the Group.

The 2 WHEELS GOOD text was turned into vector outlines before importing the design document. Each character is a separate path. You don't need to edit this text, so let's optimize this artwork using the Heads-Up Display (HUD).

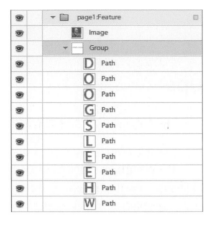

▶ **Tip:** You can also optimize graphics by choosing Modify > Optimize Vector Graphics.

4 The Group is still selected, so in the Optimize Artwork section of the HUD, click Choose Command, and choose Optimize Vector Graphics.

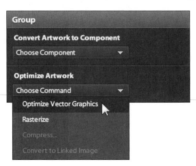

The vector paths are turned into a single object in the Layers panel named Graphic1.

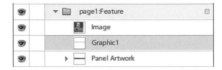

5 Change the name from Graphic1 to **2 WHEELS GOOD**.

Adding and deleting layers

Adding new layers in the Layers panel is simple; you simply add a new layer folder. To add a new top-level layer folder, click the Create New Layer icon (⊞). To add a new sublayer folder, select an existing top-level layer and click the Create New Sublayer icon (⊞). Deleting layers is just as easy. Select the layer folder and click the Delete icon (🗑). When you add or delete layer folders, the changes appear in every page state (or component state when editing a component).

1 In the Layers panel, click the Create New Layer icon (⊞).

A new top-level layer folder is added at the top of the Layers panel. New layers are named Layer1, Layer2, and so on. You can rename this layer folder, just like any other object in the Layers panel.

2 Select the new layer folder (Layer1), and click the Delete icon (🗑) in the bottom-right corner of the Layers panel.

The new layer folder is gone. If this application had more than one page, the layer would be removed from all pages. If this layer contained any objects, those objects would also be removed from every page.

► **Tip:** To remove an object from the current state without removing it from other states, select the object and press Delete.

● **Note:** If an object name appears dimmed in the Layers panel, it means the object is not present in the current state, but It does appear in another state of the application.

Stacking artwork using layers

To change the stacking order of objects in the application, you can drag rows up or down in the Layers panel. You can also change the stacking order of objects within a layer or group.

● **Note:** The stacking order of layers is constant across all states. You can't have a different stacking order in different states.

1 Look at the artboard and notice that the orange 2 WHEELS GOOD text appears over a semi-transparent gray background.

2 In the Layers panel, inside the page1:Feature layer, drag the Panel Artwork row above the 2 WHEELS GOOD row.

A gray line indicates the new location for the row when you release the mouse.

Now look at the artboard again. The orange text appears below the semi-transparent gray background and is barely visible.

3 Choose Edit > Undo to return to the proper stacking order of the artwork.

4 Expand the Panel Artwork layer.

To change the stacking order of objects within the same layer or group, you can drag rows in the Layers panel or use the Arrange commands in the Modify menu.

5 Select the Transparency BG row in the Layers panel and choose Modify > Arrange > Bring to Front.

The Transparency BG row moves to the top of the stack, but only within its parent group. You can tell by looking in the artboard that the stacking order of these objects is important to the integrity of the design.

6 Choose Modify > Arrange > Send Backward.

Each time you choose Send Forward or Send Backward the object moves up or down one row.

7 Choose Modify > Arrange > Send to Back.

The Transparent BG layer moves back to the bottom of the stack, where it belongs.

8 Drag the 2 WHEELS GOOD row into the Panel Artwork layer and position it at the top of the stack.

9 Collapse and lock the Panel Artwork layer.

There is one last change that needs to be made to the arrangement of the objects in the page1:Feature layer. The Image row, at the top of the stack, belongs inside the Sample Images sublayer folder.

10 Drag the Image row (with the picture of a man) down until it's directly over the Sample Images row. This causes the Sample Images row to expand automatically. When it does, drag the Image row above the 2 wheels image row and release the mouse button.

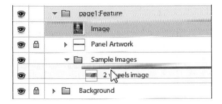

The Image row is now inside the Sample Images sublayer folder.

Review questions

1 What is the target layer, and how is it identified in the Layers panel?

2 What types of items appear in the Layers panel?

3 What does a small blue square in the Layers panel indicate?

4 In a new Flash Catalyst project, why do some rows have descriptive names, while other rows have generic names, such as Image, Graphic, or Group?

5 How can you make the Layers panel more manageable when your project includes artwork, such as illustrations or text outlines, that contains several small paths?

6 How do you change the stacking order of objects in the Layers panel.

7 When you add a bitmap image from the Library panel to the artboard, a new Image is added to the Layers panel. What happens to the image in the Library panel if you rename this object in the Layers panel?

Review answers

1   You can make any unlocked and visible layer the target layer by selecting it. When you add a new object to the artboard, either by dragging from the Library panel, by importing, by drawing shapes, or by adding new text, the new object is placed in the target layer. The target layer is identified in the Layers panel by light blue shading.

2   The Layers panel shows every object in the application using a collection of stacked rows. Rows can represent layers, sublayers, objects (images, vector drawings, text, media, and components), and groups (grouped objects).

3   A small blue square means the row includes a selected object. This is useful for finding selected items in the Layers panel when not all layers are expanded. You can follow the boxes as you drill down to find the selected item(s).

4   When you create a new Flash Catalyst project from a design document you created in Photoshop, Illustrator, or Fireworks, the naming and structure of the design document is preserved in Flash Catalyst. When you add new objects in Flash Catalyst, these new objects begin with generic names, such as Group and Image.

5   Grouping complex graphics is one way to keep the Layers panel more manageable. If you don't need to work with the individual parts of a vector graphic, you can select its parts and create a single optimized graphic. Once you do this, it becomes a reusable optimized graphic in the Library panel.

6   To change the stacking order of objects, you can drag rows up or down in the Layers panel. You can also change the stacking order of objects within a layer or group using the Arrange commands in the Modify menu.

7   There is no link between the names of objects in the Layers panel and the names of assets in the Library panel. You can change the name of objects in the Layers panel without affecting the name of the source asset in the project library.

5 WORKING WITH PAGES AND STATES

Lesson Overview

Rich Internet applications are engaging, informative, relevant, and fresh. They pack lots of dynamic content into very limited screen space. A common goal is to keep the interface simple, yet filled with information that's easy to locate, and even easier to navigate. This is done by carefully organizing your application into just a few meaningful pages or views. Then within each of those pages, you present large amounts of content using interactive components—windows, menus, lists, or panels that expand, collapse, flip, or morph in some way to show and hide information at just the right moment. In Flash Catalyst, this organization begins with pages and states.

In this lesson, you'll learn how to do the following:

- Create and name states

- Modify states by showing and hiding objects

- Add and remove objects in a specific state

- Delete objects from all states

- Delete states

 This lesson will take about 30 minutes to complete. Copy the Lesson05 folder into the lessons folder that you created on your hard drive for these projects (or create it now), if you haven't already done so. As you work on this lesson, you won't be preserving the start files; if you need to restore the start files, copy them from the *Adobe Flash Catalyst CS5 Classroom in a Book* CD.

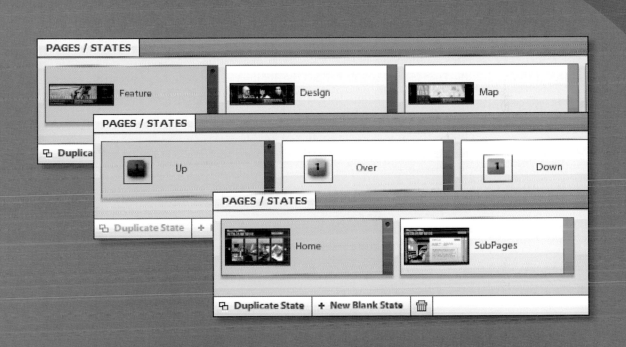

States represent how your application changes at different points in time throughout the application. As a user moves between pages, they are viewing different page states. As someone interacts with a component, they see the different states of that component. In one state a menu appears collapsed, and then in another state the same menu expands to reveal more options.

75

Page and component states

Note: Most built-in components have very specific states, such as the Normal and Disabled states of a text entry field. These states cannot be duplicated, deleted, or renamed. On the other hand, custom components are created and edited much like page states.

Most rich Internet applications present information on more than one page or screen, and each page can include various interactive components. Examples of interactive components are navigation menus, scrollable panels, buttons, multimedia controls, and so on. The different views a user sees when interacting with the application and components are called *states*. In Flash Catalyst, there are two types of states.

Page states, also referred to as pages, are the different pages or screens of the application. Page states usually represent the topmost level in the application hierarchy.

Component states are the different views or states of an interactive component, such as the Up, Over, Down, and Disabled states of a button component.

Note: When a component is being edited in Edit-In-Place mode, the Layers panel splits into sections. It shows layers for the main application and the components you are editing.

To view the different page states of the application, you simply select a page in the Pages/States panel. To view the different states within a component, you can double-click the component in the artboard to edit it in Edit-In-Place mode and view its states in the Pages/States panel.

In this lesson, you will begin to develop the page states for an interactive banner, but the same principles apply when creating and modifying the states of a custom component.

Less is more

Flash Catalyst applications can have up to 20 page states (or 20 unique states in a custom component). That may seem like a limitation, but adding too many pages to an application can slow performance, not to mention that it makes the application difficult for users to navigate.

When it comes to interface design, keep it simple. In an application, 20 pages are more than enough. Fewer is even better. Instead of creating a separate page for every unique view, you can encapsulate content into related subcategories using custom components that present the right information at just the right time. Use menus that collapse and expand, scrolling lists, or panels that flip to reveal more information. You can even nest components inside other components to create more depth and structure in the application without adding more application pages.

Duplicating and modifying page states

To add additional pages, you can duplicate and modify an existing page without creating or placing the same artwork. Duplicating page and component states ensures that common objects maintain their exact position as you move from one page or state to the next. By maintaining the exact position of objects in different states, you can prevent objects from shifting as you move from page to page or interact with a component.

Save time by duplicating page states

This project was created by importing an Illustrator file with a single artboard, so all the artwork is stacked together in the same page. This works to your advantage, because you can quickly duplicate Page1, and then show or hide the same artwork to create new pages.

Note: When you duplicate a state, you are not duplicating objects. You are creating new states that include the same objects.

1   Start Flash Catalyst. Browse to the Lesson05 folder and open Lesson05_Banner.fxp.

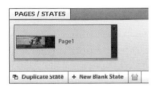

The artwork for this application was imported from Adobe Illustrator and is stacked together on Page1. Page1 is selected in the Pages/States panel.

Note: The stacking order of layers is constant across all states. You can't have a different stacking order in different states.

2   Click Duplicate State.

Flash Catalyst creates an exact duplicate of Page1. The new state is named Page2.

3   Click Duplicate State three more times to create a total of five pages.

Give page states descriptive names

Flash Catalyst names new pages Page1, Page2, Page3, and so on. You may find that giving descriptive names to pages will help you match artwork to the appropriate page. For example, if you have a top-level layer folder for each page, you can name the pages to match those folders.

Consider the following when naming pages and component states:

• State names must begin with a letter.

• State names cannot contain spaces.

• State names cannot contain special characters, such as !@#$%^&*().

Let's rename some pages:

1 Double-click Page1 in the Pages/States panel.

2 Type **Feature** and press Enter/Return.

3 Rename Page2 **Design**.

4 Rename Page3 **Map**.

5 Rename Page4 **Restaurants**.

6 Rename Page5 **Future**.

   The page names now relate to the layer folders used to organize their artwork. You can see this by comparing the Pages/States panel with the Layers panel.

Show and hide artwork in each page state

Now that you've made five copies of the same page, you can use the Layers panel to show and hide the artwork for each page.

1 In the Pages/States panel, select Feature.

   If you look in the Layers panel, you can see which layers are visible on this page. This page includes the Top Btns, Top Graphic, and Background layers, and the artwork in the page1:Feature layer. This is the correct artwork for the Feature page.

2   In the Pages/States panel, select Design.

3   In the Layers panel, click the eyeball icon to hide the page1:Feature layer and show the page2:Design layer.

This is the correct artwork for the Design page.

4   In the Pages/States panel, select Map.

5   In the Layers panel, hide the page1:Feature layer and show the page3:Map layer.

6   In the Pages/States panel, select Restaurants.

● **Note:** Any change that affects the application hierarchy is shared across all states automatically. For example, if you group objects or convert objects to components, the change applies to all states. If you edit a component, you edit the component definition in the project library. The changes apply to all instances of the component in all states.

Sharing is good

In Flash Catalyst, the Layers panel is shared by all page and component states in the application. As you move from one state to the next, the rows in the Layers panel are identical, although some objects may exist and be visible in one state, but not in others.

An object can be present in multiple states, and that object can have a completely different set of properties in each state, such as size, position, rotation, color, and opacity. Once you position and modify an object to your liking, you can quickly share that object to other states. This technique makes it possible to create smooth transitions from one state to the next. For example, you can create the effect of an object fading in or out or morphing from one shape or position to another.

- To share an object to other states, select the object and choose States > Share To State. Select the states to which you want to share the object. You can also select the target state (the one to which you'll add the object) and turn on the eyeball for the object. The object is made present and visible in the current state.

- To remove an object from a specific state, select the object in one state and choose States > Remove From State. Choose the state from which you want the object removed. You can also view the state from which you want to remove the object, select the object in the artboard, and press Delete.

- If you change the properties of an object in one state, you can quickly apply the same properties to the same object in all other states. Select the object and choose States > Make Same In All Other States.

7 In the Layers panel, hide the page1:Feature layer and show the page4: Restaurants layer.

8 In the Pages/States panel, select Future.

9 In the Layers panel, hide the page1:Feature layer and show the page5: Future layer.

10 Click through each page in the Pages/States panel to preview the look of each page in the application.

Adding and deleting states

Not every new page or component state is derived from an existing state. For example, when you begin a new blank project it opens with a blank page. You can also add new blank states to any application or custom component from the Pages/States panel. A blank state offers a clean slate on which you can design an entirely fresh layout.

Add a blank page state

New blank states are always added after the last state.

1   In the Pages/States panel, click New Blank State.

A blank page state is added to the end of the Pages/States panel, after the Future page. You may need to scroll the Pages/States panel to see the new page.

2   Rename the new page **Gardens**.

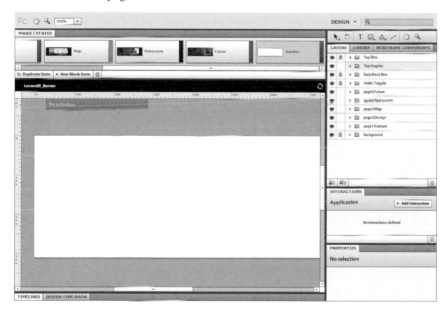

The artboard appears to be completely blank. A blank artboard can mean that every object in the current state is hidden, or that no objects are present in the current state. In the case of a new blank state, there are no objects present. It is truly blank.

3   Take a look at the Layers panel.

In a new blank state, every layer folder is made visible by default. So why don't we see any of this artwork in the new page?

4 In the Layers panel, expand the Top Graphic layer, the Page1:Feature layer, and the Panel Artwork sublayer.

All layers are visible, but the objects within those layers are not present in the current state. When an object is present somewhere in the application (in another state), but does not exist in the current state, it appears dimmed in the Layers panel.

Add objects to blank page states

You can add objects to a new blank state using a few different methods:

- Share objects from other states.
- Import new images, video, SWF files, or layered artwork from Adobe Illustrator, Adobe Photoshop, or FXG documents.
- Drag an object from the Library panel to the new blank artboard.

Let's add an object to the blank state:

1 In the Layers panel, show the TopGraphic row (the graphic object, not the parent layer).

The eyeball icon appears for this object. You have just shared or copied the graphic to the current state, as seen in the artboard.

LAYERS	LIBRARY	WIREFRAME COMPONENTS	
👁 🔒 ▶ 📁	Top Btns		
👁 ▼ 📁	Top Graphic		
👁	TopGraphic		

▶ **Tip:** Anytime a project asset appears in another state, you're better off sharing that item to a new state rather than dragging another instance from the Library panel. Each time you add an item from the Library panel, you create a new instance. If the item already exists in the application, you'll end up with duplicate objects in the Layers panel.

2 Click the eyeball icon to hide the TopGraphic object.

The graphic is hidden in the artboard, but the object's name still appears dark in the Layers panel (it's not dimmed). This means the object is still present in the current state, but now it's hidden from view.

3 Show the TopGraphic object again so the gray rectangle is visible at the top of the artboard.

4 Add a new layer in the Layers panel and name it **page6:Gardens**.

5 Drag the page6:Gardens layer so that it is positioned directly above the page5:Future layer.

6 If it's not already selected, select the page6:Gardens layer to make it the target layer (light blue) for new content.

7 Choose File > Import > Adobe Photoshop File (.psd). Browse to the Lesson05 folder, select garden.psd, and click Open. Click OK to accept the default import options.

Layered artwork from the Photoshop design document is added to the application.

8 Expand the page6:Gardens layer.

The new artwork is placed inside the target layer and is visible in the current page state.

9 Select any of the other five pages in the Pages/States panel.

The artwork you just added appears dimmed in the Layers panel for the other five pages. This artwork is only present in the new page state.

Delete objects from specific states

▶ Tip: If you want the object to fade in or out as you transition between states, then leave the object present in both states and hide it or change its Opacity to 0, instead of deleting it.

Depending on how you delete an object, it can be removed from the current state, from a specific state that you select, or from the entire application.

1 In the Pages/States panel, select Gardens.

2 Select only the TopGraphic object in the artboard. You can do this by clicking the graphic in the artboard, or by clicking the TopGraphic layer in the Layers panel.

3 Press the Delete key.

The TopGraphic object appears dimmed in the Layers panel. Pressing the Delete key removes selected objects from the current state. If the object(s) exist in other states, those instances are not affected.

4 Select any of the other five pages in the Pages/States panel.

The TopGraphic object still exists in these states.

● Note: Deleting a reusable library asset from the application (all states) does not remove it from the project library. The asset can be added again from the Library panel.

5 Return to the Gardens page in the Pages/States panel.

6 In the artboard, click to select the image with the green leaves on it (page6sm in the Layers panel).

7 Choose States > Remove from State.

A menu appears with a list of every page state in the application. A dimmed menu option means the object doesn't exist in that state. From here, you can delete objects from a specific state only.

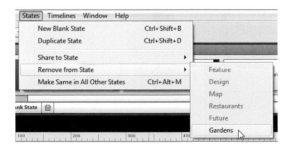

8 Choose Gardens to remove the selected image.

The image is removed from the artboard. Because this image only existed in the Gardens page, it no longer exists anywhere in the application and its row is deleted from the Layers panel.

9 In the Layers panel, select the page6:Gardens layer to select every object in this layer. This selects every remaining object in the Gardens page.

10 In the Layers panel, click the Delete icon (⌗).

When you delete an object in the Layers panel (by clicking the Delete icon), the object is removed from every state in the application.

Delete page states

To remove an entire page or component state, use the Delete icon in the Pages/States panel.

1 Make sure the Gardens page is selected in the Pages/States panel.

2 Click the Delete icon at the bottom of the Pages/States panel.

The Gardens page is removed from the application.

The blank page is gone.

Review questions

1 What is the fastest way to create a new page or component state based on an existing state in the application or component?

2 What is the maximum number of pages that you can add to a Flash Catalyst application?

3 How is new content added to a blank page state?

4 What is a fast way to copy artwork from one state to another state where that artwork is not present?

5 What does it mean when a row in the Layers panel appears dimmed?

6 What happens if you select objects in the artboard and press the Delete key?

7 How can you remove selected objects from every state of the application with a single click?

Review answers

1 You can quickly create a new page or component state based on an existing page. Duplicate the existing page in the Pages/States panel and use the Layers panel to show or hide artwork in the new state.

2 Each Flash Catalyst application can have up to 20 page states, but fewer is better. Whenever possible, consider adding new views or screens by creating custom components. You can even create components that exist within other components.

3 There are a few ways to add new content to blank pages. You can drag assets from the Library panel, import new assets, or share assets from another state in the application.

4 When artwork exists in the application, but is not present in the current state, the artwork appears dimmed in the Layers panel. By clicking the Show/Hide box in the Layers panel, you add a copy of the object to the current state.

5 A dimmed row in the Layers panel represents an object that exists in the application in another state, but is not present in the currently selected state.

6 When you select objects and press the Delete key, those objects are removed from the current state only. If those objects exist in other states, they are not affected.

7 You can delete selected objects from the entire application (every state) by clicking the Delete icon (🗑) in the Layers panel.

6 CREATING INTERACTIVE COMPONENTS

Lesson Overview

You've seen them in just about every computer application—a window that scrolls, options in a dialog box, menus and buttons that take you from one page to the next. These and other interactive elements are the building blocks of applications. In Flash Catalyst they're called *components*.

In this lesson, you'll learn how to do the following:

- Use wireframe components for rapid prototyping
- Convert artwork to built-in components
- Create custom navigation and toggle buttons
- Create custom scroll bars and scrolling panels
- Build custom components and navigation buttons
- Add and format text
- Modify components using Edit-In-Place mode
- Share artwork between component states
- Add and delete Flash Catalyst interactions

 This lesson will take about 90 minutes to complete. Copy the Lesson06 folder into the lessons folder that you created on your hard drive for these projects (or create it now), if you haven't already done so. As you work on this lesson, you won't be preserving the start files; if you need to restore the start files, copy them from the *Adobe Flash Catalyst CS5 Classroom in a Book* CD.

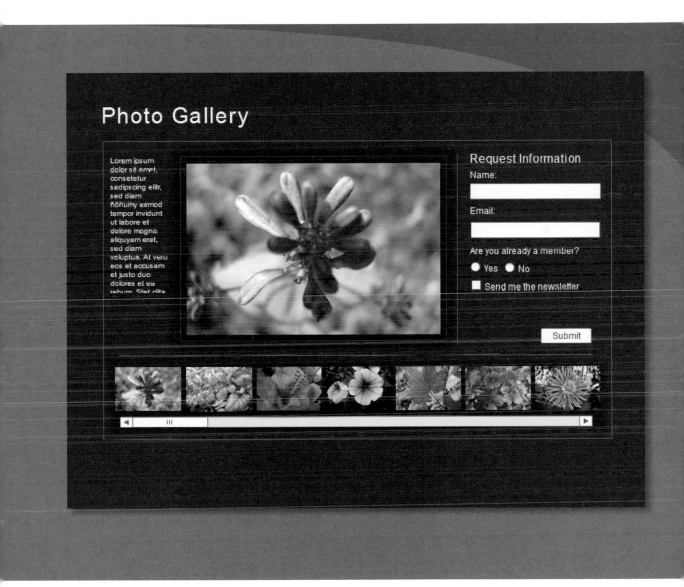

Design interactive components, like scroll bars, buttons, and sliders. Begin with ready-to-use wireframe components, or convert your custom artwork to one of several built-in components, and then add interactivity like page navigation, UI controls, and links.

The building blocks of RIAs

The building blocks of rich Internet applications (RIAs) are components and the interactions that bring them to life.

Components

Flash Catalyst provides a collection of components with built-in states and behaviors, such as the up, over, down, and disabled states of a simple button. You can also create a custom component where you define the states and behavior from scratch. You can even create components that include other components. For example, you can have a scroll panel that includes a scroll bar and buttons.

Creating components

There are a few different ways that you can add a Flash Catalyst component to your application. These include:

- Drag wireframe components with a generic appearance from the Wireframe Components panel.

- Convert artwork into one of several built-in components (button, check box, and so on).

- Convert artwork to make a custom component.

Using Edit-In-Place

▶ **Tip:** When editing components in Edit-In-Place mode, the Layers panel divides into separate sections for the main application layers and the component layers. You can drag objects from the main application into the component and vice versa.

After adding a component to the artboard, you can edit the component using Edit-In-Place and modify its individual parts. When using Edit-In-Place, you are editing the component's definition in the project library. The changes apply to every instance of that component in every state of the application. This is different than applying properties. When you select a component and change its properties in the Properties panel, the properties apply only to the current state. To apply the same properties to the component in all other states, you can select the component and choose States > Make Same In All Other States.

Interactions

You can add Flash Catalyst *interactions* that define a desired behavior when a user interacts with a component (or grouped artwork). An interaction is like a set of instructions that tells the program what to do in response to a user event, such as clicking a button.

Using wireframe components

Most likely you'll want to design custom user interface elements. But for rapid application prototypes or for simple functions like submitting a form, use the Flash Catalyst wireframe components.

The built-in wireframe components are ready-to-use and fully functional user interface elements. They can be used "as is" or quickly modified to your liking.

Flash Catalyst includes ten built-in wireframe components with a generic *skin* or appearance. These include:

- Button
- Checkbox
- Data List
- Horizontal/Vertical Scrollbar
- Horizontal/Vertical Slider
- Radio Button
- Text Input
- Toggle Button

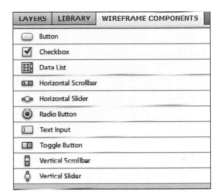

Add and modify wireframe buttons

Adding a wireframe component to your application is easy. Just drag a component from the Wireframe Components panel to the artboard.

1   Start Flash Catalyst. Browse to the Lesson06 folder and open the flower_gallery.fxp file.

    This is a prototype for an online photo gallery. It includes some placeholder images and text. The next step is to add some basic interactive components.

2   Open the Library panel.

    Notice there is no Components category. Right now this project doesn't include any components.

3   Open the Wireframe Components panel.

▶ **Tip:** If the Timelines and Design-Time Data panels are open, collapse them so that you can see more of the artboard.

4 Drag a Button component from the Wireframe Components panel to the artboard. Position the button below the Request Information text, just above the thumbnail images.

The button has a default label of Button. You can see the label on the button itself and in the Common category of the Properties panel. In the Properties panel, the current *skin* for this button is Wireframe. This means that it's using the generic wireframe artwork for the button. Skin refers to the artwork or set of instructions that defines the graphical representation of the button.

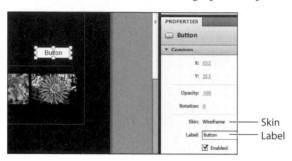

5 Open the Library panel again, and notice there is still no Button component in the library.

This is because you added a wireframe component, and there's no reason to place another copy in the project library. It's available in the Wireframe Components panel already. For minor customization, you can change its properties in the Properties panel, but if you edit the button it becomes a new skin in the Library panel. This is done to preserve the original wireframe and so that you can reuse your edited button in other parts of the application.

6 With the button still selected, double-click the Label field in the Common category of the Properties panel. Type **Submit** and press Enter/Return.

The label on the button changes to Submit.

7 Double-click the button or click Up in the Heads-Up Display (HUD).

The button is in Edit-In-Place mode. Everything except the button is dimmed in the artboard. The component states appear in the Pages/States panel, and the Breadcrumbs bar shows that you are editing the Button component.

Breadcrumbs bar   Button component states   Button in Edit-In-Place mode

8   Open the Layers panel.

When a component is being edited, its layers are added to the Layers panel. The wireframe button includes three objects—a label and two rectangles. In the Up state, only the bottom rectangle is present.

Button components all have Up, Over, Down, and Disabled states. You can tell by looking in the Pages/States panel that you cannot change the states of a Flash Catalyst built-in Button component. The Duplicate State, New Blank State, and Delete buttons are inactive. However, you can modify the objects in each of its existing states.

9   In the Pages/States panel, change to the Over state.

10 In the artboard or in the Layers panel, select the visible rectangle. Be careful not to select its label.

▶ **Tip:** Sometimes it's easier to isolate and select small parts using the Layers panel, especially when there are overlapping parts.

11 In the Common category of the Properties panel, click the Fill Color swatch to open the Color Picker and select a new color from the palette.

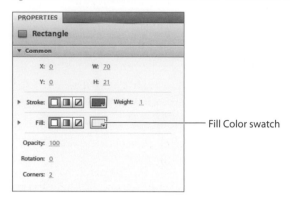

Fill Color swatch

The Over state of the button changes color.

▶ **Tip:** You can also use the Breadcrumbs bar or double-click anywhere in the dimmed part of the artboard to exit Edit-In-Place mode.

12 Press Esc to exit Edit-In-Place mode.

13 Open the Library panel again.

This time the Library panel includes a Button component. This is because you edited the wireframe button in Edit-In-Place mode, which creates a new skin (based on the wireframe) automatically.

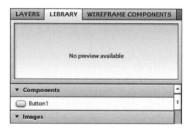

In the Properties panel, the skin for this button now refers to the name of the new component, Button1, in the Library panel.

Add wireframe text input fields

There are some components that you probably don't need to customize. A text input field used in a form is a good example.

1 Change back to the Wireframe Components panel and drag a Text Input component to the artboard. Position it below the text that reads "Name."

   As long as you haven't edited a wireframe component, it can be sized using the selection handles or by changing its Height (H) and Width (W) values in the Properties panel.

2 In the Common category of the Properties panel, change the Width (W) of the Text Input field to **180**. You can type the new value.

> ▶ **Tip:** Using the Max Characters property in the Properties panel automatically sizes a Text Input field to accommodate a specific number of characters. This is only applicable when a wireframe text input field has not been manually sized.

3 Expand the Text category in the Properties panel.

   You can format the text that appears when someone types in the text field. These default settings are fine.

> ▶ **Tip:** If you select the Display As Password property in the Properties panel, the text input field's contents appear as a series of asterisks when someone types in the field. This is used to protect the secrecy of passwords.

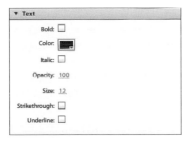

4 Drag another Text Input component below the text that reads "Email." Using the selection handles, widen the Email field to match the Name field.

> ▶ **Tip:** When you place the pointer over a value in the Properties panel, it turns into a two-headed arrow. You can drag across the top of the value to change it. Dragging to the right increases the value. Dragging to the left decreases the value.

> ▶ **Tip:** You can use the Align options on the Modify menu to align one component relative to another.

Add wireframe radio buttons

Radio buttons, also known as option buttons, typically present a choice for users. These choices are mutually exclusive and the user must choose only one option. For example, you may have a form that asks a yes or no question, or you may want someone to rate something by selecting from a group of options. When you add radio buttons to the application, each button represents an option. The user can select only one option at a time.

1   In the Wireframe Components panel, drag a Radio Button component to the artboard and place it below the text that reads "Are you already a member?"

    The blue text is hard to read over the dark background.

2   In the Properties panel, change the radio button's label to **Yes** and change the color of the text to white.

3   Add another Radio Button component next to the first one. Change its label to **No** and change the text color to white.

> **Tip:** To present multiple questions and choices using radio buttons, group each set of radio buttons or assign them to a common group using the Radio Button Group property in the Properties panel.

Only one radio button within a group of radio buttons can be selected. Radio buttons are in the same group when:

• Their Radio Button Group property is set to the same name in the Properties panel.

• The buttons have been selected and grouped by choosing Modify > Group.

• They are all part of the same component.

• They exist at the main application level (as in this example).

Add a wireframe check box

Check boxes are used when answering a question is optional, or when a user can select more than one option in a list. Each check box is independent of the others. Typically a single check box is used for a single option that the user can turn on or off, opt in, opt out, and so on.

1   In the Wireframe Components panel, drag a Checkbox component to the artboard. Position it directly below the two radio buttons.

2   In the Properties panel, change its label to **Send me the newsletter**.

3 Double-click the check box to edit it in Edit-In-Place mode.

Notice in the Pages/States panel that a Checkbox component has a different set of Up, Over, Down, and Disabled states for when it's selected.

4 In the artboard, click to select the check box label "Send me the newsletter."

5 In the Common category of the Properties panel, change the text color to white.

6 In the HUD, click the Make Same In All Other States option.

The white text property is copied to all states in the component. That's a huge time-saver.

7 In the Pages/States panel, select the Selected,Up state (not the Up state) and change the text color in the Properties panel to bright yellow.

Now the text is white until someone selects the check box, then it turns yellow.

8 Press Esc to exit Edit-In-Place mode.

This prototype needs one last wireframe component—a scroll bar for the list of thumbnails.

Add wireframe scroll bars

All scroll bars in Flash Catalyst must include a track and a thumb. The track runs the length or height of the scrollable area. The thumb is used to scroll content along the track. Optionally, you can include up and down buttons (vertical scroll bars) or left and right buttons (horizontal scroll bars).

1 In the Wireframe Components panel, drag a Horizontal Scrollbar component to the artboard. Position it directly below the thumbnail images.

The default width of the horizontal wireframe scroll bar is 200. As long as you don't plan to edit the wireframe scroll bar, you can size it using the handles or the Properties panel.

Note: If you edit the scroll bar in Edit-In-Place, it becomes a custom skin. You can no longer control its size in the Properties panel. To size a custom scroll bar, you need to edit the size of its parts in Edit-In-Place mode.

2 Using the selection handles or the Properties panel, change the width of the scroll bar to match the width of the thumbnails. In the Properties panel, this is about W:660.

3 Choose File > Run Project to run the project and view the new components in a web browser.

4 In the web browser, type something in the Name and Email fields. Select a radio button, and select the check box. Roll over and click the Submit button, and test the thumb and scroll arrows of the scroll bar.

When you select the check box, the text turns yellow. The scroll bar is not attached to any content yet, so you won't see the thumbnails move.

5 Close the browser window and return to Flash Catalyst.

6 Save and close the flower_gallery.fxp project.

Note: If the Tab To Focus component property is deselected, pressing tab will not give the component keyboard focus. It must be clicked to get focus.

▶ **Tip:** When you run the project, the focus changes from one component to another as the user presses Tab or clicks to select a component. Focus is indicated by a subtle blue highlight called the focus ring. The focus ring color can be changed in the Appearance section of the Properties panel. You can also change the Tab order of the objects on a page by changing their Tab Index property in the Component section of the Properties panel. Lower numbers place the item earlier in the sequence. The –1 indicates a default order, which is based on the order of objects in the Layers panel.

Sliders vs. scroll bars

You may be wondering when it's best to use a Slider component versus a Scrollbar component.

Scroll bars are best for scrolling an area of the screen or a group of content up and down or from side to side. Use scroll bars to fit lots of information in a small space.

Sliders let users set contiguous values, such as volume or brightness. A slider is a good choice when the value is a relative quantity, not a fixed numeric value. For example, a slider can be used to control changes to the hue, saturation, or luminosity values of an image. A slider is a good option when you want to give users control over a relative setting and allow them to see the effects of their change immediately.

In Flash Catalyst, you can use the Horizontal and Vertical Slider components in the Wireframe Components panel or design your own by converting artwork. Once you add a slider in Flash Catalyst, a developer can add the desired functionality using Adobe Flash Builder.

Converting artwork to built-in components

Wireframe components are convenient, but the real magic happens when you begin to transform your well-crafted original artwork into rich interactive user interfaces.

Flash Catalyst provides 11 types of built-in components that you can customize using your own artwork. But if the built-in components don't fit your needs, you can use the Custom/Generic Component option to design additional components with up to 20 unique states.

The built-in component types include:

- Button
- Checkbox
- Radio Button
- Toggle Button
- Text Input
- Horizontal Slider
- Vertical Slider
- Scroll Panel
- Horizontal Scrollbar
- Vertical Scrollbar
- Data List
- Custom/Generic Component

When you convert artwork to a component, Flash Catalyst stores the new component in the Library panel, creates a new component object in the Layers panel, and replaces your artwork with an instance of the new component in the artboard.

> **Tip:** To create a new component based on an existing component, right-click the component in the Library panel and choose Duplicate.

Some components have special requirements and will not function properly until you define their required parts. For example, a Data List component must have a repeating item, and a scroll bar must have a track and a thumb. If the component has special requirements, a message appears in the HUD with instructions on how to complete the component.

> **Tip:** To rename a component in the Library panel, right-click the component and choose Rename. Type a new name and press Enter/Return.

Skinning components

The terms *skin* or *skinning components* refer to the visual appearance or graphics that define the look of a component.

Skins can define the visual appearance of individual parts of a component or the entire component in its various states. For example, a button control can have many skins, each representing a state of the button.

Flash Catalyst allows for easy skinning of components. When you convert your artwork to a built-in component using the HUD, you are skinning, or adding graphics to, the underlying component without writing any code.

Convert artwork to buttons

To design buttons with a custom appearance, select the artwork for the Up, Over, and Down states of the button. Then, convert the artwork to a Button component. Edit the component and use the Layers panel to show or hide artwork in each state.

1   If necessary, start Flash Catalyst. Browse to the Lesson06 folder and open the Lesson06_Banner.fxp file.

2   In the Layers panel, expand the page1:Feature layer, and then expand the Panel Artwork group.

3   Use the Layers panel to select the Visit The Feature Article and Triangle objects. You can Ctrl-click/Command-click to select both rows.

Artwork selected in the artboard and in the Layers panel

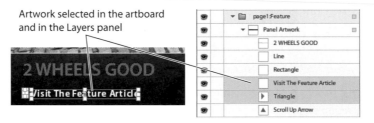

4   In the Convert Artwork To Component section of the HUD, click Choose Component, and then select Button.

The selected objects are turned into a single Button component in the Layers panel.

5 In the HUD, click Over to edit the button in Edit-In-Place mode.

The Over state is selected in the Pages/States panel. The Layers panel includes the objects used to create the button.

6 In the Layers panel, click to select Visit The Feature Article.

The text is selected in the Layers panel and in the artboard.

7 In the Common category of the Properties panel, change the text color to orange.

8 Press Esc to exit Edit-In-Place mode.

9 Run the project and test the new button.

When you roll over the button, the text turns orange. Later in this lesson, you will use this button to link to another web page.

10 Close the browser, return to Flash Catalyst, and lock the page1:Feature layer.

Tip: When creating buttons from small text, add a transparent rectangle to define a larger clickable area. The larger transparent shape makes the button much easier to use. Make sure that Transparency Accepts Mouse is selected in the Properties panel. If it's not selected, all mouse actions will pass through the transparent areas to the layers below the component.

Create a reusable navigation button

Any button can be used for navigation, including wireframe buttons. If your navigation buttons look the same, you can use repeated instances of the same button. For example, in the interactive banner application, the navigation buttons at the top of the window are identical except for their labels. Instead of creating five new buttons, create one button that you can use five times. You can change the label in each instance using the Label property.

1 In the Layers panel, unlock and expand the Top Btns layer.

These buttons are placeholders to show you how the final navigation should look. You will use one of these objects to make a reusable navigation button, so you can delete the repeated artwork.

2 In the Layers panel, select the Btn 5, Btn 4, Btn 3, and Btn 2 objects. Ctrl-click/Command-click to select multiple rows.

3 Click the Delete icon (🗑) in the Layers panel (not the Delete key on the keyboard) to remove these objects from all states.

4 In the Layers panel, click the Btn 1 object to select the layer and all of its contents.

Tip: You can Shift-click to select a contiguous range of objects in the Layers panel.

The Btn 1 artwork is selected in the artboard. You may want to zoom in on the artboard to see this artwork close-up. About 200% should do it.

5 In the Convert Artwork To Component section of the HUD, click Choose Component, and then select Button.

6 In the HUD, click Up to edit the button in Edit-In-Place mode.

7 In the Layers panel, expand the Btn 1 layer and the group within it.

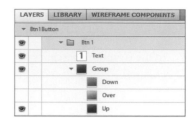

The button includes text and the artwork for each state of the button. You need to convert the Text object into a button label so that you can change the number on each instance of the button.

8 Click the Text object in the Layers panel to select the text.

● **Note:** Defining a label part in a button is an optional step, but it allows you to easily change the text label for each instance of the button by modifying its Label property.

9 In the Convert To Button Part section of the HUD, click Choose Part, and then select Label.

In the Layers panel, the text object changes to Label. Next, you need to define the appearance in each state of the button. To do this you will select each state and then show and hide artwork in the Layers panel.

10 Make sure the Up state is selected in the Pages/States panel and the Up row is visible in the Layers panel.

11 Select the Over state in the Pages/States panel. In the Layers panel, hide the Up row and show the Over row.

12 Select the Down state, hide the Up row, and show the Down row.

13 Select the Disabled state, hide the Up row, and show the Down (orange) row.

You're using the orange Down button as the Disabled state so that you can disable a button in any state to make it appear selected (orange). You can disable a button in the Properties panel.

14 Press Esc to exit Edit-In-Place mode.

The next step is to add additional instances of the button to the artboard.

15 Open the Library panel and use the Preview window to locate the new button in the Components category. It will be called something like Btn1Button.

16 Drag another instance of the button from the Library panel to the artboard and place it beside the first button.

The label will read "Button" until you define it in the Properties panel for each instance.

17 In the Properties panel, enter **2** in the Label field.

18 Repeat steps 16 and 17 to add and label buttons 3, 4, and 5.

19 Use the alignment options or the arrow keys to fine-tune the position of the buttons.

20 In the Pages/States panel, select the Design page.

Notice that you've only added the new buttons to the Feature page. That's OK because you can quickly share the new buttons to every state.

21 Change back to the Feature state, then drag to select all five navigation buttons in the artboard.

22 With all five buttons selected, choose States > Share To State > All States.

Now all states include the five buttons.

23 Choose Edit > Deselect All to deselect the five buttons.

▶ **Tip:** You can support users with impaired vision by adding accessible text to buttons and other objects. Use the Accessible Text property in the Properties panel to add descriptive text that's recognizable by screen reader technologies.

Enable and disable buttons

Here's a great trick. You've seen navigation buttons that appear different than the others when they're selected. It's a nice feature because it helps orient the user to where they are in the application.

Flash Catalyst Button components don't have a "selected" state that indicates which button or page is currently selected. But you can use the Disabled state for this purpose.

1 Make sure the Feature page is selected in the Pages/States panel.

2 Select the first navigation button. Then, in the Properties panel, deselect the Enabled property.

The button in the artboard turns orange because this is the look you defined in the Disabled state. Now when someone views page 1 (the Feature page), the button is orange to show them which page they're on.

3 In the Pages/States panel, change to the Design page. Select the second navigation button and use the Properties panel to disable it.

4 Change to the Map page, select the third button, and disable it.

5 Change to the Restaurants page, select the fourth button, and disable it.

6 Change to the Future page, select the fifth button, and disable it.

7 In the Layers panel, collapse and lock the Top Btns layer.

8 If you zoomed in earlier, then zoom back out to see more of the artboard.

Create next and previous buttons

In the interactive banner application, the positions of the Back and Next buttons change from page to page. Because of this, you'll need to make large and small versions of each button. The artwork for these buttons is included in the Back/Next Btns layer.

1 Make sure you are still viewing the Future page, the last page. Unlock and expand the Back/Next Btns layer. Show the layers for all four Back/Next buttons.

You need to show the buttons so that you can select them.

Grouped artwork for —
the Back/Next buttons

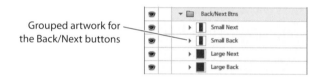

2 Select the Small Next layer.

This includes the artwork for the smaller of the two Next buttons.

3 In the HUD, convert the selected artwork to a Button component.

4 In the HUD, click Up to edit the button in Edit-In-Place mode.

5 In the Layers panel, expand the Small Next layer to see the artwork for this button. Hide the Orange layer in the Up state.

The button begins with a semitransparent arrow that turns orange when you roll over it.

6 Exit Edit-In-Place mode.

A new button replaces the artwork in the Layers panel.

7 In the Layers panel, rename the new button **Small Next**.

8 Repeat steps 2 through 7 for the other Back/Next buttons. After turning them into buttons, rename them **Small Back**, **Large Next**, and **Large Back**.

Artwork converted to —
Button components

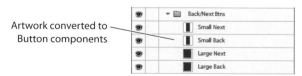

9 In the Future page, use the Layers panel to show the Large Back button and hide the other Back/Next buttons.

The other four pages already have the correct buttons showing and hidden.

10 Collapse and lock the Back/Next Btns layer.

Create a custom toggle button

Toggle buttons are typically used to trigger simple on/off functions. For example, you can use a toggle button to turn music on and off or play and stop a video. The interactive banner application requires a toggle button to play and stop the videos that you'll add later to pages 4 and 5.

1 In the Pages/States panel, select the Restaurants page.

2 In the Layers panel, show, unlock, and expand the Video Toggle layer.

The artwork for the toggle button includes pause and play symbols and a semitransparent orange circle.

3 Click the Video Toggle layer to select all the artwork for the toggle button.

4 In the HUD, convert the artwork to a Toggle Button component and then click Up to edit the component in Edit-In-Place mode.

Toggle buttons have eight states that cannot be duplicated, added to, or deleted. There are two sets of Up, Over, Down, and Disabled states—one for when the button is in its initial state, and another for when the button is selected.

5 In the Layers panel, expand the Video Toggle layer.

6 Hide the Pause symbol in the Up, Over, and Down states.

7 In the Disabled state, hide the Toggle Button layer so that the entire button is invisible when disabled.

8 Hide the Play symbol in the Selected,Up, Selected,Over, and Selected,Down states.

9 In the Selected Disabled state, hide the Video Toggle layer to make it invisible.

10 Press Esc to exit Edit-In-Place mode.

The new button is visible on page 4, the Restaurants page.

11 Select the Future page, the last page, and show the toggle button.

The toggle button needs to be moved a little to the right on this page. Objects, including components, can have their own unique set of properties in each state (including position), so moving the button here will not affect its position on the previous page.

12 Drag the toggle button so that it's centered in the photograph.

▶ **Tip:** You can change the position of components in the artboard by using their X and Y coordinates in the Properties panel.

13 Lock the Toggle Button row in the Layers panel.

Convert artwork to scroll bars

You can quickly turn your graphics into vertical and horizontal scroll bars of any size. You can use just about any artwork. The only rule is that you have to include a track and a thumb. The up, down, right, and left scroll buttons are optional. The parts of a scroll bar can be positioned anywhere, on or off the artboard.

1 In the Pages/States panel, select the Feature page.

2 In the Layers panel, unlock and expand the page1:Feature layer and its Panel Artwork group (if they're not already expanded).

The Panel Artwork group includes the artwork for the lower design panel of this page, including the vertical scroll bar that you'll use to scroll a block of text.

3 In the Layers panel, Ctrl-click/Command-click to select the following four objects: Scroll Up Arrow, Scroll Down Arrow, Thumb, and Scroll Track.

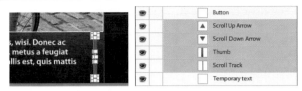

4 Use the HUD to convert the selected artwork to a Vertical Scrollbar component.

The Auto Change Warning message appears telling you that selected objects have interactions or effects attached. You're getting this message because the objects are present in more than one state so Flash Catalyst added some default transitions between states.

5 Click OK to continue.

A message in the HUD reminds you that to make the scroll bar work correctly, you need to assign its parts. Flash Catalyst needs to know which artwork to use as the thumb and the track.

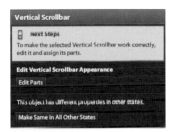

6 Click Edit Parts in the HUD to edit the scroll bar in Edit-In-Place mode.

7 Select the artwork for the Thumb (thin vertical orange rectangle).

▶ **Tip:** When editing a component with small parts, you can zoom in on the artboard for a closer view.

8 In the Convert To Vertical Scrollbar Part section in the HUD, click Choose Part, and then select Thumb.

9 Select the artwork for the Scroll Track (thin vertical black rectangle).

10 In the HUD, click Choose Part, and then select Track.

The message in the HUD goes away. You have defined all of the required parts (track and thumb) for a Scrollbar component.

11 Select the artwork for the Scroll Up Arrow (top orange triangle). Using the HUD, convert this part to the Up button. Convert the Scroll Down Arrow (bottom orange triangle) to the Down button.

12 Drag the Up and Down buttons away from the track and the thumb.

You can position the parts of a Scrollbar component anywhere you want.

13 Run the project and test the scroll bar by dragging its thumb and clicking the up and down arrows. Also, try clicking and holding the up and down arrows.

14 Close the browser window and return to Flash Catalyst.

15 Select the Up and Down buttons (orange triangles). Use the Delete icon in the Layers panel to remove them from all states.

This scroll bar looks better without the Up and Down buttons.

16 Press Esc to exit Edit-In-Place mode.

You can set properties to control the distance that content scrolls when using the scroll bar. When a scroll bar is selected, these properties appear in the Properties panel.

Page Size controls how far the thumb moves in a scroll bar when clicking in the track.

Step Size controls how far the thumb moves when clicking the arrows. In a slider, Step Size controls how far the thumb moves when pressing the arrow keys.

Snap Interval forces the thumb in a scroll bar to snap in increments rather than moving smoothly. Page Size and Step Size are always forced to be multiples of the Snap Interval.

Can I make a scroll bar with no track or thumb?

Technically, every Scrollbar component must have a track and a thumb. But suppose you want a pair of buttons (up and down or left and right) that scroll a range of content without the use of a track and a thumb.

Fortunately, you can place the parts of a scroll bar anywhere you want. As long as the scroll bar includes a track and a thumb, it will work.

1 Create a scroll bar with a track, a thumb, and buttons (up/down or left/right). Edit the Scrollbar component in Edit-In-Place mode.

2 Drag the track and thumb parts below or to the side of the artboard, so they are not visible to the user.

3 Position your scroll buttons where you want them in the artboard.

When you run the project, this creates the illusion of a scroll bar with no track and no thumb.

Work with text

Flash Catalyst includes a tool for adding text. This is mainly intended for creating labels or short blocks of text. Flash Catalyst is not the best place to generate large amounts of copy. A better workflow is to write and edit your copy in another application, such as Microsoft Word, and then copy and paste the spell-checked, edited, and approved copy into your Flash Catalyst design.

1 Make sure the Feature page is still selected.

2 Select the Temporary Text object in the Panel Artwork group of the page1:Feature layer.

This is just placeholder text.

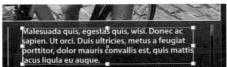

3 Use the Delete icon () in the Layers panel to remove the temporary text from all states.

4 Select the Text tool in the Tools panel, and drag to create a text box in the empty area to the left of the vertical scroll bar (where you deleted the temporary text). Make it large enough so that it extends below the artboard.

You are extending the text box below the artboard because you're going to create a scrolling panel of text. The text box needs to be large enough for the scrolling text. It doesn't have to be exact, because you can resize it later.

5 The new text box includes a flashing insertion point. Type some text in the new text box.

As you type, the text is constrained to the text box. The default text properties are a little hard to see over the dark background, but you'll fix that in a minute.

6 Choose File > Save to save your project, and keep it open.

7 Minimize or hide the Flash Catalyst window. Open the panel_text.txt file in the Lesson06 folder. You can use any word processor to open the text file.

8 Select and copy the block of text that begins with "What do architectural landmarks..." and ends with "...bicycle tour of Meridien."

9 Change back to the Flash Catalyst window.

10 Drag to highlight the text you added in the text box. Press Delete to remove the text but not the text box. If you accidentally delete the entire text box, then create a new one.

The flashing insertion point should be in the top-left of the text box.

11 Choose Edit > Paste to paste the text you copied from the text document.

When you paste text from another application, any formatting is lost. If there is too much text to fit in the text box you drew, you can resize it. Use the Select tool to drag the text box selection handles.

12 Using the Text tool, select the pasted text, and then use the Properties panel to format the text. Make it white and choose any other formatting that you prefer.

The text should still extend below the artboard. In the next exercise, you will create a scrolling panel to display the text.

13 In the Layers panel, drag the new Text object into the Panel Artwork group and place it just above the Vertical Scrollbar.

👁		☐	Button
👁		☐	Text
👁		☐	Vertical Scrollbar
👁		☐	Transparency BG

Use the right text for the job

There are three types of text that you can add in Flash Catalyst.

Point Text does not line wrap. The text box extends to fit all of the text. You can press Enter/Return to insert a line break.

Area Text occupies a bounding box with fixed width and height. The text never grows any larger than the width and height you specify. Text automatically line wraps, but you can also enter manual line breaks. If the text does not fit within the box, the remainder is hidden. An overflow icon appears at the bottom of the bounding box. Clicking the overflow icon changes the text to Fit Height. The bounding box height adjusts automatically.

Fit Height text occupies a box with fixed width but variable height. The text stays within the width of the bounding box. Text automatically wraps. You can also insert manual line breaks. The height of the box grows automatically, if needed, to fit all the text.

- Clicking the Text tool in the artboard places the insertion point and creates Point Text.

- Dragging the Text tool in the artboard creates Area Text. There are two ways to resize the text bounding box. Double-clicking inside the box reveals four selection handles. Drag the handles to resize the box. Or, use the Select or Direct Select tools to select the text bounding box. Selecting the box reveals eight selection handles. Drag the handles to resize the bounding box.

- Resizing Fit Height text converts it to Area Text.

- To change a text object from one type to another, use the Select or Direct Select tool to select the bounding box. In the Properties panel, choose Point Text, Area Text, or Fit Height.

Create a scroll panel from artwork

A common challenge in web design is finding space in the available window to display all the necessary content. One solution is to create scrolling panels. A panel creates a well-defined container for content in the user interface. By adding scrolling content and a scroll bar, you can place a large amount of information in a limited space. To create a scroll panel component in Flash Catalyst, you need:

- An object that will scroll, such as a long block of text or a series of images
- A scroll bar for scrolling the content
- An object to define the panel area, such as a rectangle shape (optional)

● Note: You can create a scroll panel without a scroll bar, but it's useless unless users can scroll to see the hidden content.

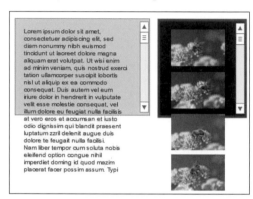

1 In the Layers panel, select the Text and Vertical Scrollbar objects.

By selecting the objects in the Layers panel, you are able to select the two parts of the scroll panel without selecting any of the other artwork in the artboard.

👁			Button
👁			Text
👁			Vertical Scrollbar
👁			Transparency BG

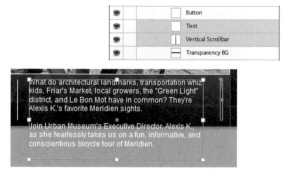

2 In the HUD, convert the selected artwork to a Scroll Panel component.

The Auto Change Warning message appears telling you that selected objects have interactions or effects attached. You're getting this message because the objects are present in more than one state so Flash Catalyst added some default transitions between states. If you don't get the Auto Change Warning message, then you can skip step 3 below.

3 Click OK to continue.

A message in the HUD informs you that to make the scroll panel work correctly, you need to assign its required parts.

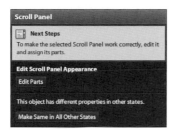

4 In the HUD, click Edit parts.

5 Select Text in the Layers panel. In the HUD, click Choose Part, and then select Scrolling Content.

In the artboard, the text block changes to a scrolling content part. The bounding box of the text is sized to match the scroll bar. You can use the selection handles to resize the scrolling text.

6 If necessary, size and position the scrolling text box so that it fits within the blank space to the left of the vertical scroll bar.

7 Press Esc to exit Edit-In-Place mode and run the project to test the scroll panel. Use the vertical scroll bar to move the text up and down.

8 Close the browser and return to Flash Catalyst.

Creating custom components

To create a custom component, you select the objects that you want to appear in the various states, and then choose the Custom/Generic Component option in the HUD. There are no required parts in a custom component, and they can include images, drawings, text, grouped objects, and other components.

Embedding or nesting a component within another component is a good way to create additional views in the same page.

Sometimes, you'll have components with only one state. By combining several objects into a single component, they can be manipulated as a single element. For example, you can apply global properties such as opacity and rotation, or create a transition that begins with a panel of objects offscreen and then have it slide into view.

1   Choose Edit > Deselect All to make sure nothing is selected in the artboard.

2   In the Layers panel, make sure the page1:Feature layer is expanded, and click Panel Artwork to select every object in the group.

This group includes all the artwork for the lower design panel on the Feature page. This includes the orange text, Featured Article button, scroll panel, white lines, and semitransparent background.

3   In the HUD, convert the selected artwork to a Custom/Generic Component.

In the Layers panel, the Panel Artwork group is now a single component object.

4   In the Layers panel, rename the new component **Feature Panel**.

5   In the HUD, click State 1 to edit the new component in Edit-In-Place mode.

▶ **Tip:** When a custom component includes more than one state, you can set its default state by selecting the component in the artboard, opening the State pop-up menu in the Properties panel, and choosing a default state.

The new custom component has only one state, as seen in the Pages/States panel. Custom components begin with all artwork on a single state, but you can duplicate or add up to 20 states, and then modify them as needed.

6   Press Esc to exit Edit-In-Place mode.

7   In the artboard, drag the Feature Panel component to the space below the artboard.

By making this into a custom component, you can manipulate it as a single object.

8   Click Edit > Undo to return the panel to its original position (aligned bottom left).

9   Collapse and lock the page1:Feature layer.

Adding interactivity

Interactions are events that occur in response to a user action, such as the click of a button. Flash Catalyst has many built-in interactions that you can quickly add to components or grouped objects. These include:

- Play a transition from one page or component state to another
- Trigger an action sequence, such as playing a sound, moving an object, or playing an animation
- Go to a URL
- Play, pause, or stop a video clip

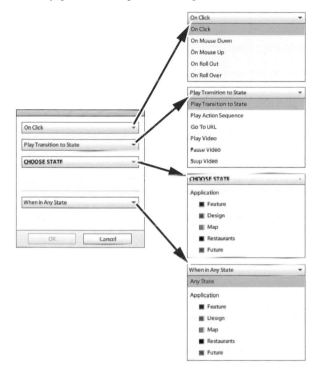

Events used to trigger an interaction include:

- On Click
- On Mouse Down
- On Mouse Up
- On Roll Out
- On Roll Over

To add interactions you must either create a component or group the artwork. Use groups to hold interactions when you don't need a reusable component.

Add page navigation

Adding page navigation is easy. First you'll need an object that will be used to hold the interaction. This can be any component or grouped artwork, but it's usually a button you've designed specifically for navigation. Select the navigation object, and then add interactions that transition from one state to another when an event occurs. Interactions are added in the Interactions panel.

1 In the Layers panel, unlock the Top Btns layer.

2 In the artboard, click to select the first button, labeled 1.

   This button will transition the application to the Feature page.

3 In the Interactions panel, click Add Interaction.

   On Click and Play Transition To State are already selected.

4 Click Choose State, and then select Feature.

   This button has the same behavior in every state. Its default setting is When In Any State.

▶ **Tip:** To modify an interaction, double-click its description in the Interactions panel, make changes, and click OK.

5 Click OK.

   A new interaction is added to the panel. When the button is clicked, the application will transition to the Feature state.

6 In the artboard, click to select the second button, labeled 2.

▶ **Tip:** If you make a mistake and want to delete an interaction, select it in the Interactions panel, and click the Delete icon in the Interactions panel.

7 Add an On Click interaction that transitions to the Design state.

8 Select button 3. Add an On Click interaction that transitions to the Map state.

9 Select button 4. Add an On Click interaction that transitions to the Restaurants state.

10 Select button 5. Add an On Click interaction that transitions to the Future state.

11 Run the project and test the top navigation buttons.

12 Close the browser window and return to Flash Catalyst.

13 Lock the Top Btns layer.

Create conditional interactions

Conditional interactions are behaviors predicated upon some condition. For example, clicking a Next button takes the user viewing page 1 to page 2, and the user viewing page 2 to page 3. Conditional interactions are added just like any other interaction. The only difference is that you change the conditional setting from When In Any State to something more specific.

1 Unlock and expand the Back/Next Btns layer.

2 In the Pages/States panel, select the Feature page (the first page).

The Large Next button is visible on this page only and navigates to the Design page.

3 Select the Large Next button.

4 In the Interactions panel, click Add Interaction.

5 Click Choose State, and then select Design.

6 Click When In Any State, and then select Feature.

7 Click OK.

This is a conditional interaction. When someone clicks the button while in the Feature state, the application transitions to the Design page. This button is only present in the Feature page, so it only needs one interaction.

8 Change to the Design page and select the Small Next button.

The Small Next button is visible on the Design, Map, and Restaurants pages. It needs to perform differently in each state.

9 Add an On Click interaction that transitions to the Map state when in the Design state.

10 With the Small Next button still selected, add another On Click interaction that transitions to the Restaurants state when in the Map state.

11 Add a third On Click interaction that transitions to the Future state when in the Restaurants state.

The Small Next button now includes three conditional interactions.

12 In the Layers panel, select the Small Back button.

13 Add an On Click interaction that transitions to the Feature state when in the Design state.

14 Add an On Click interaction that transitions to the Design state when in the Map state.

15 Add an On Click interaction that transitions to the Map state when in the Restaurants state.

The Small Back button now includes three conditional interactions.

16 Change to the Future page (the last page) and select the Large Back button.

This button is only visible in the Future page.

17 Add an On Click interaction that transitions to the Restaurants state when in the Future state.

18 Run the project and test the Back/Next buttons on each page.

The same buttons perform differently, depending on which page you're viewing.

19 Close the browser window and return to Flash Catalyst.

20 Collapse and lock the Back/Next Btns layer.

Conditional list interactions

You can add conditional interactions to a data list that trigger an action when someone selects a specific item in the list. The list can include images or text. Conditional list interactions are similar to other interactions. The difference is that the conditional setting, When In Any State, becomes When Any Item Is Selected or When A Specific Item Is Selected. If you choose When A Specific Item Is Selected, you enter the number of the item in the list as the condition for the interaction.

Link to external content

Navigation isn't limited to the current application. You can also add interactions that open external content.

The interactive banner application includes links on each page that point to additional external information, such as an article or an interactive restaurant guide.

1 In the Pages/States panel, select the Feature page.

2 In the Layers panel, unlock the page1:Feature layer.

3 In the artboard, double-click the Feature panel at the bottom of the artboard to edit the custom component in Edit-In-Place mode.

4 In the Layers panel, expand the Panel Artwork group and select the Button object.

   This selects the button you created earlier.

5 In the Interactions panel, click Add Interaction.

6 Click Play Transition To State to open the menu, and choose Go To URL.

   A field appears below the Go To URL interaction. This is where you add the URL.

7 Click in the empty field and type **www.adobe.com** (or a different URL of your choice).

8 Click Open In Current Window, and then select Open In New Window.

9 Click OK.

This button now links to the URL you entered.

10 Press Esc to exit Edit-In-Place mode and run the project.

11 In the browser window, test the link by clicking the button.

The URL you entered opens in a new browser window.

12 Close the browser and return to Flash Catalyst.

13 Save and close the project.

On application start interactions

Not all interactions are initiated by user events such as clicking a button. You can also include interactions that happen automatically when the application starts.

For example, you may want a video or SWF movie to begin playing automatically. Or, you can define a default page state by creating an On Application Start interaction that goes to a specific state when the application opens.

On Application Start interactions are added in the Interactions panel. Make sure nothing is selected in the artboard, and click Add Interaction. When nothing is selected in the artboard, the event is set to On Application Start. It's the only option available.

Review questions

1 What is the difference between the built-in wireframe components and the built-in component options in the HUD?

2 What happens to a wireframe component after it has been edited in Edit-In-Place mode?

3 What are the required parts in a Flash Catalyst Scrollbar component?

4 What is the best type of component for collecting answers to yes or no questions?

5 How can the Disabled button state and the Enabled button property be used together to help orient users to which page or state is currently selected?

6 What types of objects can be used to trigger an interaction?

7 What is a conditional interaction?

Review answers

1 The wireframe components are ready to use "as is" and include a generic skin or appearance. The built-in components in the HUD require that you provide the artwork for the new component.

2 When you edit a wireframe component in Edit-In-Place mode, the component becomes a new skin in the Library panel. The component can no longer be sized using the Properties panel.

3 A Flash Catalyst Scrollbar component must have a track and a thumb. The up, down, left, and right buttons are optional.

4 Radio buttons are best for presenting choices that are mutually exclusive. The user must choose only one option.

5 When a button is used to navigate to a specific state, you can format the button's Disabled state to appear selected or highlighted, and then disable the button in the target state.

6 Interactions can be added to components or grouped artwork. You can also create On Application Start interactions that occur automatically when someone starts the application.

7 Conditional interactions are behaviors predicated upon some condition. For example, clicking a Next button takes the user viewing page 1 to page 2, and the user viewing page 2 to page 3. Conditional interactions are added just like any other interaction. The only difference is that you change the conditional setting from When In Any State to something more specific.

7 CREATING TRANSITIONS AND ACTION SEQUENCES

Lesson Overview

We've come to expect a lot from our online experience. With the introduction of high-quality streaming video and motion graphics, the boundaries between film, television, and the web are fuzzier than ever. As an application designer, your audience has come to expect similar production quality. We can learn a lot from film and television. Talk to any film or video producer and they'll tell you that much of what shapes our viewing experience are the subtle things we're not even aware of—lighting, ambient sound, and of course transitions. Placing smooth animated transitions between the pages and states of your application can change the entire user experience.

In this lesson, you'll learn how to do the following:

- Preview default transitions

- Add smooth transitions between states

- Fine-tune transition timing and other properties

- Add special effects to transitions

- Add and modify action sequences

- Preserve the fidelity of transitions as you edit the project

This lesson will take about 45 minutes to complete. Copy the Lesson07 folder into the lessons folder that you created on your hard drive for these projects (or create it now), if you haven't already done so. As you work on this lesson, you won't be preserving the start files; if you need to restore the start files, copy them from the *Adobe Flash Catalyst CS5 Classroom in a Book* CD.

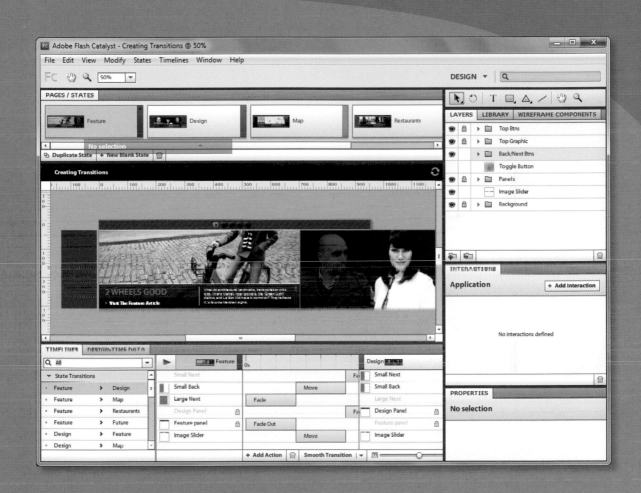

Reproducing film-like transitions in web applications used to be a very time-consuming, specialized task for computer animators. But with the introduction of Flash Catalyst, you can now produce smooth, professional-looking animated transitions with just a few clicks of the mouse.

Transitions and action sequences

Transitions are animations that play once as the user moves from one page or component state to another. Transitions are made up of special effects called actions that define the transition. For example, transitions can include simple fades, as well as animated effects like rotating objects in 3D or resizing images.

Action sequences are interactions that trigger one or more actions. Action sequences can be added to components or groups. Action sequences occur within a single state, so they can play over and over. For example, you may have an object that animates each time a user moves the pointer over it.

The types of actions, or effects, that are available include:

- Play, pause, or stop a video
- Control the playback of a SWF movie
- Set the component state
- Set the properties of an object
- Fade an object
- Add a sound effect
- Move, resize, or rotate an object
- Rotate an object in 3D

You work with transitions and action sequences in the Timelines panel.

State Transitions   Timeline

Time-based animation

Flash Catalyst transition effects are created using time-based animation.

Animation is a change in position over time. Reposition an object several times per second and it creates the illusion of movement.

There are two ways of doing this: moving the object a specific number of pixels based on the current frame (frame-based), or moving the object based on time (time-based). The playback of frame-based animation has the potential to be affected by a user's browser or system performance, whereas time-based animation will produce more consistent and predictable results in different environments.

Inspecting default transition effects

Anytime the content in one state differs from the content in another state, default transition effects are added to identify those changes. The default transition effects start out with durations of zero seconds, so they're really more like placeholders. You bring them to life by increasing their duration.

You can view and edit transitions in the Timelines panel. The types of effects (Fade, Move, and so on) in each transition will vary depending on the objects in each state and how each object differs from one state to another.

Let's start by taking a look at how the default transitions appear when you run the application. Knowing which content exists in each state will help you edit transitions more effectively.

1   Start Flash Catalyst, browse to the Lesson07 folder on your hard drive, and open the Lesson07_Banner.fxp file.

    The interactive banner application includes five page states, as seen in the Pages/States panel.

2   Choose File > Run Project to view the project in a browser.

    The first page includes background images and a semitransparent panel at the bottom. The panel includes graphics, a button, and scrolling text. This page also includes navigation buttons (at the top) and a side navigation button (on the right).

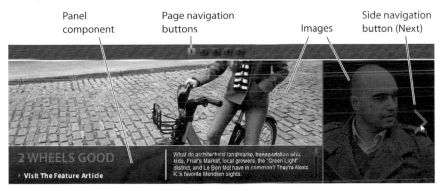

Panel component | Page navigation buttons | Images | Side navigation button (Next)

3   Use the top or side navigation buttons to view each page in the application.

    Each page includes a different set of images and a similar-looking panel at the bottom. The last two pages include a play/pause toggle button. These pages will include video.

    Notice that as you move from one page to the next, the change happens very quickly. What you're seeing (or not seeing) are the zero-second default transition effects.

4 Close the browser and return to Flash Catalyst.

5 Select the Image Slider layer in the Layers panel.

The Image Slider custom component is selected in the artboard.

6 Use the Zoom Magnification box to change the zoom to 25%.

The Image Slider is a single-state custom component that combines the images for each page. In the Feature page, it's positioned so that the Feature images are visible in the artboard, but the other images are out of view. In the Properties panel, the Image Slider is positioned at X:0 (left-aligned) and Y:36 (36 pixels from the top).

7 Select the Design page in the Pages/States panel.

The Image Slider is positioned differently in the artboard to display the Design images.

8 Select each page in the Pages/States panel, and notice which panel layers are visible or hidden. Also pay attention to the position of the Image Slider component in the artboard.

9 Choose Edit > Deselect All to deselect the Image Slider.

10 Change the artboard view to 66% magnification. If necessary, scroll the workspace so the artboard is visible.

11 Open the Timelines panel at the bottom of the Design workspace.

The Timelines panel shows every transition in the application.

12 Select Feature > Design in the State Transitions section of the Timelines panel.

The Feature page is the start state of the transition, and the Design page is the end state. Default transition effects are added for each change that occurs between the start and end states. Default transitions have durations of zero seconds.

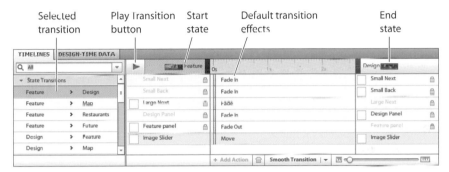

The default effects for this transition include five fades and one move:

- The Small Next and Small Back buttons start out hidden in the Feature page and become visible in the Design page.

- The Large Next button is visible in the Feature page, but hidden in the Design page.

- The Design panel fades in as the Feature panel fades out.

- The Image Slider, which is visible in both states, moves to a new position.

13 Click the Play Transition button.

The transition is instantaneous, due to the zero-second effect durations.

Adding smooth transitions

Adding smooth transitions is easy. You simply change the duration of the effects from zero seconds to something a little longer, making the transition visible when you run the application.

1 Make sure the Feature > Design transition is still selected in the State Transitions section of the Timelines panel.

2 Click the small arrow beside the Smooth Transition button.

The Smooth Transition Options dialog box appears. These are the default settings that apply to all selected transitions when you click Smooth Transition. These settings persist after changing them. For this exercise, you are going to set them to the defaults.

Duration sets the overall time of the transition from start to end.

Simultaneous applies smooth transitions to each effect equally, using the value you set in the Duration field. Each effect begins and ends at the same time.

Smart Smoothing adjusts the duration and delay (start time) of each effect, creating a series of staggered effects. The effects play at different times over the duration you specify. Flash Catalyst uses a logical order for effects, beginning with objects fading out. After objects fade out, all resize and move effects play, followed by objects fading in.

Overwrite Existing Effects applies the new settings to your existing transitions.

▶ **Tip:** You don't need to open Smooth Transition Options each time you set smooth transitions. Clicking Smooth Transitions applies your most recent settings automatically.

3 Make sure the duration is set to **.5** sec (a half second). Make sure the Simultaneous option is selected, and that Overwrite Existing Effects is not selected. Click OK.

The default transition effects are extended to .5 seconds, creating smooth transitions between the start and end states. A small green dot appears beside the transition to show that it has been modified.

Edited transition

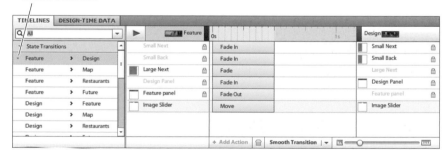

4 Click the Play Transition button at the top of the Timelines panel to see the smooth animated transition effects. Play the transition a few times to see the different types of effects.

Fade effects create the appearance of objects fading in or out of view. This is similar to a film dissolve between two scenes. The Image Slider begins in one position and moves to its end position, revealing a new set of images in the Design page.

● **Note:** A Fade In transition begins when an object is hidden or not present in the start state and becomes visible or present in the end state. A Fade Out transition is the opposite. Sometimes Flash Catalyst can't identify the effect perfectly, so it labels the Effect bar Fade.

You can quickly apply smooth transitions between every page state in the application.

5 In the State Transitions section of the Timelines panel, click to select the Feature > Map transition (the second one in the list).

You can see in the Timeline that this transition also includes default zero-second transition effects.

6 Hold down the Shift key, scroll to the bottom of the State Transitions list, and click the Future > Restaurants transitions (the last one in the list).

This selects every remaining transition in the application.

7 Click Smooth Transitions in the Timelines panel.

Now every transition in the application includes smooth .5-second transition effects.

8 Run the project in a browser and use the navigation buttons to view the smooth transitions between page states.

9 Close the browser and return to Flash Catalyst.

Fine-tuning transitions

If you've applied smooth transitions using the Simultaneous option, your transition effects begin and end at the same time. The effects overlap, and one effect may overpower, hide, or detract from the others. You can fine-tune transitions by controlling when each effect begins and ends. This is done using a combination of duration and start time (delay). These two simple controls give you the power to choreograph complex animations, controlling the pace, flow, and tone of the entire user experience.

Adjust transition duration

Each transition has an overall duration. This is defined by the start of the first effect and the end of the last effect. You can adjust the duration of each individual effect by dragging its resize handle or by changing its duration value in the Properties panel.

1   Select Feature > Design in the State Transitions section of the Timelines panel (the first transition in the list).

2   Click the green Effect bar of the Move transition effect to select it.

    This is the effect that moves the Image Slider to its new position in the Design page.

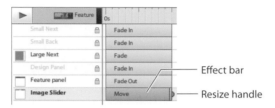

Effect bar

Resize handle

When a transition effect is selected, its Effect bar turns blue and its properties appear in the Properties panel. These include the duration of the transition, delay (when the transition begins), and easing. You'll learn about easing transitions in a moment.

3   Drag the Move Effect bar resize handle to the left to shorten the duration of the transition. Drag the handle to the right to lengthen the transition.

    As you drag, a tool tip shows the new duration of the effect.

4   In the Properties panel, set the Duration value to 1 second.

5   Run the project and view the transition between pages 1 and 2.

    The Image Slider takes longer to move between pages—1 second to be exact. Compare this to the timing of other transitions as you move from page to page.

6 Close the browser and return to Flash Catalyst.

7 Make sure the Move Effect bar is still selected (blue) in the Timeline.

8 Click the Delete icon (🗑) at the bottom of the Timelines panel.

The duration returns to zero seconds. You can't remove a default transition effect from the Timeline, but by changing its duration back to zero it becomes virtually non-existent.

9 Choose Edit > Undo to restore the 1-second duration of the Move effect.

Change transition timing

Transition timing refers to its start and end times. You can control the start time of an effect by dragging its Effect bar in the Timeline or by changing its Delay value in the Properties panel.

1 Drag the Effect bar (not the handle) of the Design Panel Fade In effect to the right.

As you drag the Effect bar, a tool tip shows the start and end times of the effect. This Start time is equal to the Delay value.

2 In the Properties panel, set the Delay value to .5 seconds.

Now the Design panel will fade in when the Image Slider is halfway completed with its move.

Delaying the transition effect can make it difficult to see in the Timeline. You can fix this by adjusting the viewing scale in the Timeline.

3 If necessary, drag the slider at the bottom of the Timelines panel to the left to compress the Timeline scale until you can see all the effects.

4 Run the project and view the transition between pages 1 and 2.

The Image Slider moves into place as the Feature panel fades out and the Design panel fades in.

5 Close the browser and return to Flash Catalyst.

▶ **Tip:** You can repeat a fade effect to emphasize or draw attention to an object. To do this, select the Fade Effect bar in the Timeline, select Repeat in the Properties panel, and set the number of times you want the effect to repeat itself.

Ease transitions

When you apply easing to effects, you are changing how those effects behave over time. The default behavior is a constant rate of change or velocity of motion between the start and end of the effect. The object begins moving at full speed and maintains that speed until it stops abruptly at the end of the transition. This is unrealistic. In real life, an object needs some time to get up to speed and then slows down before coming to a stop. If an object stops suddenly, it may bounce back before settling into its final position.

You can achieve more realistic-looking movements by applying *easing* to your effects. Easing consists of two phases: the acceleration, or *ease in* phase, followed by the deceleration, or *ease out* phase.

Easing is added in the Properties panel, and there are several easing options:

- **Default** applies a constant rate of change from start to finish.

- **Linear** starts out slow, quickly easing into the effect. It then maintains a constant rate until just before the end of the effect when the rate slows down, easing out of the effect.

- **Sine** eases in, accelerates to a midpoint, and then immediately begins decelerating, or easing out.

- **Power** is similar to Sine because it eases in to a point and then begins easing out. But with the Power option, you can also set the Exponent property. A higher exponent value creates greater acceleration and deceleration.

- **Elastic** causes a moving object to snap back and jiggle once it reaches its destination.

- **Bounce** causes the moving object to reach its destination and then bounce backward before settling into its final position.

Let's apply easing:

1 Click to select the Move Effect bar for the Image Slider in the Timeline.

2 In the Properties panel, open the Easing pop-up menu and choose Linear.

The Linear easing properties are added in the Properties panel. You can change the amount of easing (in or out) by entering new values or by dragging the handles below the diagram.

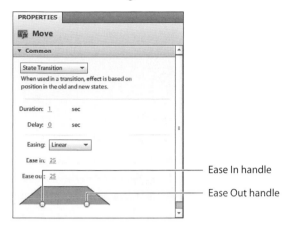

3 Click the Play Transition button.

The Image Slider accelerates, moves along at a constant speed, and then decelerates to its final stopped position.

● **Note:** The end result of changing easing properties is very subtle and may be difficult to see.

4 Apply the Bounce easing property to the Image Slider Move effect, and then click the Play Transition button to see how this looks.

▶ **Tip:** Achieving perfect easing usually involves some trial and error.

Adding and changing effects

As you've seen, default effects are added to each state transition based on the presence, visibility, or properties of objects in the start and end states. If you make changes to the objects in the start or end states, the default transitions update automatically.

You cannot remove the default transition effects, but in some cases you can add more than one effect to the same object. For example, if an object fades or moves, you can add an additional effect that causes the object to rotate.

Swap one effect for another

To swap one effect for another, you need to change the presence, visibility, or properties of the object in either the start or end state of the transition. For example, to change a fade to a move, you make the object visible in both states (removing the fade), and then place the object in different start and end positions (adding the move).

To see how this works, let's change the Small Back button transition from a Fade In to a Move effect so that it slides into view from the left of the artboard.

1   Make sure the Feature page is selected in the Pages/States panel and the Feature > Design transition is still selected in the State Transitions section of the Timelines panel.

The Back/Next Btns layer is locked. When an object is locked in the Layers panel, it is also locked in the Timeline. To change or apply new effects to an object, you need to unlock it.

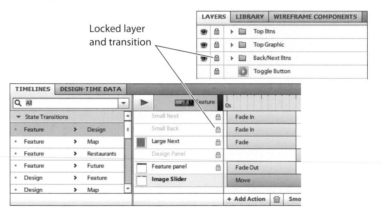

2   In the Layers panel, unlock and expand the Back/Next Btns layer.

The Small Back button is hidden in the Feature page and visible in the Design page, creating the Fade In effect.

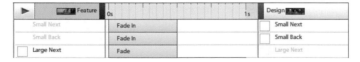

3   In the Layers panel, show the Small Back button in the Feature page.

The Small Back button now appears in both the start and end states, so the Fade In transition disappears from the Timeline.

4 In the Layers panel, click Small Back to select the navigation button in the artboard.

The Small Back button (semitransparent rectangle) is selected in the artboard. You know it's selected because it's surrounded by a blue outline and has a small blue square in the center.

5 Hold down the Shift key, and drag the Small Back button to the left until it's off the artboard.

Holding down the Shift key as you drag left or right prevents the object from moving up or down. As soon as you drag the object to a new position in the start (or end) state of the transition, a new Move effect is added to the transition automatically. The new transition has a duration of zero seconds.

▶ **Tip:** You can also Shift-drag an object up or down to prevent the object from moving left or right.

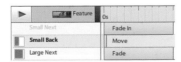

6 In the Timeline, click the new Move effect to select it. Then drag its resize handle or use the Properties panel to change its duration to .5 seconds.

7 Run the project to view the effect in a browser.

The Small Back navigation button (on the left) slides into view as you move to the Design page.

8 Close the browser and return to Flash Catalyst.

Add multiple effects to the same object

You may want to apply more than one change to an object during the same transition. There are two ways to do this. You can make additional changes to the object in the start or end state of the transition, or add new effects from the Add Actions menu in the Timelines panel.

1 In the Layers panel, hide the Small Back row in the Feature page state.

A Fade In effect is added to the Small Back button in the transition. This object now has two effects applied to it: a fade and a move.

This will look better without the fade, so let's go ahead and remove it.

2 Select the Fade In Effect bar for the Small Back object (the one you just added).

3 Click the Delete icon (🗑) at the bottom of the Timelines panel.

The Fade In Effect bar is still there. To remove this effect, you need to make its visibility identical in both states.

4 In the Layers panel, show the Small Back row in the Feature page state.

The effect is removed from the transition in the Timeline. The Small Back button will move but not fade.

You can also add effects from the Add Action menu at the bottom of the Timelines panel.

5 Select the Restaurants page in the Pages/States panel.

This page includes a pause/play toggle button. The same button appears in the Future page, but in a different position.

6 In the State Transitions section of the Timelines panel, select the Restaurants > Future transition.

In this transition, the Toggle Button object starts in one position in the Restaurants page and moves to a new position in the Future page.

7 Unlock the Toggle Button object in the Layers panel.

8 In the Timelines panel, click the Toggle Button transition to select it.

The Add Action button at the bottom of the Timelines panel becomes active.

9 Click Add Action to open the pop-up menu, and choose Rotate 3D.

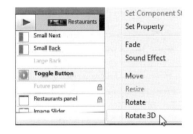

A Rotate 3D Effect bar is added to the Timeline and its properties appear in the Properties panel. You can adjust the duration and timing of this effect, just like other transitions. You can choose to rotate the object in three dimensions. The default setting is to rotate the object 360 degrees (one rotation) around a vertical axis.

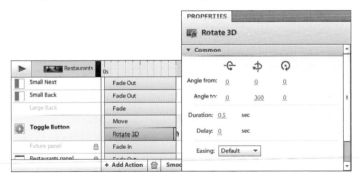

10 Click the Play Transition button in the Timeline to preview the new transition effects.

Now the toggle button rotates as it slides into its new position in the Future page. Sometimes the best way to get the exact effect you want is to experiment with different settings in the Properties panel.

11 Experiment by changing the properties for the Rotate 3D effect in the Properties panel. After setting a new property, click the Play Transition button to see the effect of each change.

12 Run the project and view the new effects in a browser.

The toggle button moves and rotates in 3D when you go from the Restaurants page to the Future page.

13 Close the browser and return to Flash Catalyst.

Adding action sequences

Whereas a transition is used to define one or more effects that occur as the application transitions from one state to another, an *action sequence* is used to apply one or more effects to an object in a single state. For example, you can use an action sequence to move an option around the artboard and cause it to rotate, change color, and fade, all while in the same state.

An action sequence is a type of interaction, so it can be triggered by a user event, such as clicking a button, or it can be triggered automatically when the application starts. Because an action sequence occurs within a single state, it can play over and over. For example, an object can animate each time a user moves the pointer over it.

Add effects with a purpose

Having too many complex transitions or action sequences can result in application performance issues at runtime, not to mention that they can overwhelm or distract users.

Each time you think about adding an effect, ask yourself this question, "Does it add something important to my application?"

Use effects when needed to define the pace or tone of the application, but resist the temptation to create special effects simply for the fun of it.

If you're confident that an effect is a positive addition to the user experience or improves usability, then it's probably worth including.

Add an action sequence interaction

Action sequences can be added to components or grouped objects in the Interactions panel.

1 Select the Future page in the Pages/States panel.

2 Select the orange play/pause toggle button in the artboard.

3 In the Interactions panel, click Add Interaction.

4 Click On Click to open the pop-up menu, and choose On Roll Over.

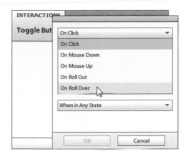

5 Click Play Transition To State to open the pop-up menu, and choose Play Action Sequence.

6 Click OK.

An empty action sequence is added to the Timeline. You can now add one or more effects from the Add Actions menu.

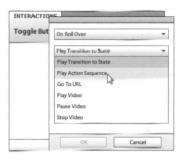

● **Note:** To add an action sequence to a component or group within another component, double-click the parent component to edit it in Edit-In-Place mode.

Edit an action sequence in the Timeline

After adding an empty action sequence interaction, you can edit it in the Timelines panel by adding one or more effects.

1 Select the Toggle Button On Roll Over action sequence in the Timelines panel.

2 Click Add Action to open the pop-up menu, and choose Rotate 3D.

The Rotate 3D effect is added to the Timeline for the action sequence.

3 Run the project to preview the action sequence in a browser. Navigate to the Restaurants (page 4) or Future (page 5) pages and roll over the play/pause toggle button to see the button rotate. The effect can play repeatedly because the effect occurs in one state at a time. The effect plays in any state where the Toggle Button object is visible.

Flash Catalyst helper effects

In some cases, making changes to objects that are currently part of a transition can negatively affect the appearance of the transition. Flash Catalyst adds additional "helper" effects to adjust for your changes and correct the transition automatically. The added effects appear as yellow Effect bars and a message appears in the Heads-Up Display (HUD) to let you know that Flash Catalyst has added the extra effects to preserve the fidelity of your transitions.

Here's an example of what you will see in the HUD:

> "This group has children with different properties in other states. Extra effects were added to your timelines to make them play correctly."

Some examples of edits that may require helper effects include:

- Grouping objects after they've been used in a move transition effect.

- Moving a group (or its children on one side of a transition).

Follow these rules to preserve the fidelity of transitions with helper effects:

- If you change the Delay value of a transition, change the Delay value for the yellow Effect bar to match. The original Effect bar and the yellow Effect bar must stay in sync.

- Do not manually change the duration of a yellow Effect bar. Flash Catalyst will adjust the yellow Effect bar duration if necessary.

A yellow Effect bar is a helper effect added by Flash Catalyst

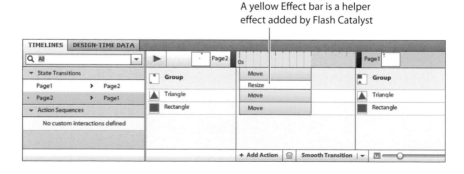

Review questions

1 What causes Flash Catalyst to add a default transition effect to the application?

2 How do you change the default settings for smooth transitions?

3 What does the Simultaneous smooth transition option do?

4 How do you change the duration of a transition effect?

5 What effect property lets you control the acceleration and deceleration of an object as it moves from start to finish during a transition?

6 How do you add multiple effects to the same object in a transition?

7 What is the difference between a transition and an action sequence?

Review answers

1 When an object in one state is not present or visible or has different properties (position, opacity, and so on) in another state, a transition effect is added between the two states.

2 You change the default settings for smooth transitions by clicking the arrow beside the Smooth Transition button in the Timelines panel. This opens the Smooth Transition Options dialog box.

3 The Simultaneous smooth transition option applies smooth transitions to each effect equally, using the value you set in the Duration field. Each effect begins and ends at the same time.

4 You can change the duration of a transition effect by dragging the Effect bar resize handle, or by changing the Duration value in the Properties panel.

5 You can achieve more realistic-looking movements by applying easing to your effects. Easing consists of two phases: the acceleration, or *ease in* phase, followed by the deceleration, or *ease out* phase. When you apply easing to effects, you are changing how those effects behave over time.

6 To add additional effects to an object in a transition, you can make additional changes to the object in the start or end state of the transition, or add new effects from the Add Actions menu in the Timelines panel.

7 Transitions are effects that play between two states. An action sequence is an interaction that plays within a single state. You can add an interaction to components or grouped objects to trigger one or more effects. Action Sequence interactions can be played over and over because they exist within the same state.

8 ADDING AND CONTROLLING VIDEO AND SOUND

Lesson Overview

Web video is everywhere—news, sports, entertainment, e-commerce, corporate communications, education, blogs, and social networking are a just few examples. Thanks to sites like YouTube and Hulu, more and more people are going directly to the web for their daily dose of information, and they expect to be entertained.

In this lesson, you'll learn how to do the following:

• Prepare video for the web

• Import video and sound

• Preview video and sound

• Add video to an application

• Control video playback

• Add sound effects

 This lesson will take about 60 minutes to complete. Copy the Lesson08 folder into the lessons folder that you created on your hard drive for these projects (or create it now), if you haven't already done so. As you work on this lesson, you won't be preserving the start files; if you need to restore the start files, copy them from the *Adobe Flash Catalyst CS5 Classroom in a Book* CD.

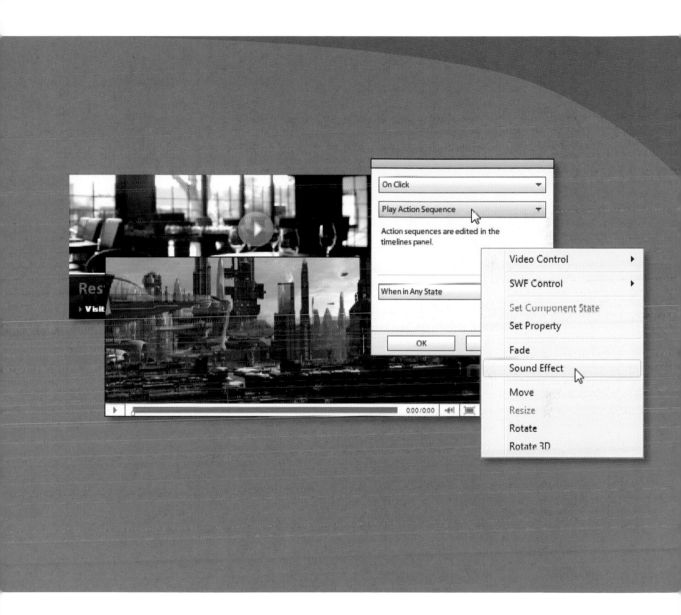

With higher bandwidth Internet connections, many web surfers have come to expect video and sound with each and every visit to the Internet.

Preparing video for the web

Most web browsers have Adobe Flash Player installed, making it easier than ever to include Flash video files (FLV and F4V) in a web page. But before you can add video to your rich Internet applications, you must *encode* it for web delivery.

What is encoding?

In Flash Catalyst, *encoding* involves converting your final edited video footage to a format compatible with Adobe Flash Player. Flash Catalyst supports FLV and F4V video files. FLV and F4V are container formats for Flash video. FLV files generally contain video data that is encoded using the On2 VP6 or Sorenson Spark codec and audio data encoded using an MP3 audio codec. F4V files generally contain video data that is encoded using an H.264 video codec and the AAC audio codec.

What is a video codec?

A *codec* is an encoding/decoding algorithm that controls how video files are compressed during encoding, and decompressed during playback.

- **H.264** is an MPEG-4–based standard for web delivery. H.264 is recommended for a variety of devices, including high-definition (HD) video, 3GPP cell phones, video iPods, and PlayStation Portable (PSP) devices.

- **On2 VP6** is the standard codec for encoding Flash video (FLV) files for Flash Player 8 and higher.

- **Sorenson Spark** is the required video compression format for Flash Player 6 and 7.

- **MP3** is a standard file format on the Internet and on many portable digital audio players.

- **Advanced Audio Coding (AAC)** is a standardized encoding scheme for digital audio. Designed to be the successor to the MP3 format, AAC generally achieves better sound quality than MP3 at similar bit rates.

How do I encode my video?

There are several applications that you can use to create FLV and F4V files, including Adobe Flash Professional CS5, Adobe Premiere Pro CS5, Adobe After Effects CS5, Adobe Media Encoder, and Sorenson Squeeze.

Each of these programs includes many presets, so most editors will not need to adjust any parameters when preparing their video for the web. You can simply select a format (FLV/F4V) and choose from a collection of presets, such as *Web - Medium Quality for Flash 8 and higher*. When you choose a preset, the video and audio codec and other settings are set automatically, including picture size, frame rate, bit rate, and so on. You can also begin with a preset, and then modify individual settings, if needed.

Whenever possible, encode a file from its uncompressed form. If you convert a file that has already been compressed using a different format, and then recompress that file into the FLV or F4V format, the previous encoder can introduce video noise.

To explain each format's unique characteristics goes well beyond the scope of this course. For more information on preparing video for the web, visit the Adobe Developer Connection Video Technology Center online at www.adobe.com/devnet/video.

Shooting web-friendly video

Shooting and editing video like a professional is now possible for anyone with an up-to-date computer, an inexpensive digital video camera, and editing software like Adobe Premiere Pro CS5. With today's digital video tools, you too can say, "Standby camera, standby talent, roll tape, ACTION!"

We've all seen examples of good and bad video on the web. The quality and style of your original footage affects how well the final video plays on the web. Here are a few suggestions for shooting web-friendly video:

- **Use a tripod to reduce camera movement**. A steady camera reduces the number of pixels that change from frame to frame, giving you better quality when the video is compressed for the web.

- **Use good lighting**. Poor lighting will produce visual "noise" on each frame of the image, making it difficult to create a quality web version of the video.

- **Use the best camera available**. The better the source image, the better the final compressed image. Cameras with an analog signal on magnetic tape (VHS, Hi-8, and so on) produce more video noise. Still-image cameras in "movie mode" have limited quality. At a minimum, shoot the source video on a digital video (DV) camera. Even consumer DV camcorders can produce decent results for web video.

- **Edit your footage**. Unless you've shot your footage directly to a computer hard drive using a tapeless workflow, editing begins by capturing or transferring your footage from your camera or digital video recorder to a hard drive. With your video converted to computer files, you can edit the footage using a desktop editing program such as Adobe Premiere Pro CS5. Editing gives you the power to transform hours of material into concise, cohesive, web-friendly stories. Editing software also gives you the ability to add transitions, color correction, filters, effects, and titles. But remember to keep it simple for the web. Once your video is edited, it's ready to encode to FLV or F4V and add to your Flash Catalyst project.

Importing and previewing video and sound

Adding motion video can turn an otherwise dull site into something engaging and memorable. The first step to adding video or sound to an application is importing the media files into your Flash Catalyst project.

Flash Catalyst supports video files with the .flv and .f4v filename extensions and audio files with the .mp3 filename extension.

Import video and sound

When you import a single video file, a new Video Player object is created in the target layer and added to the artboard. The source video is stored in the project library. When you import more than one video file, or an audio file, the files are stored in the library until you decide to use them.

1 Start Flash Catalyst, browse to the Lesson08 folder on your hard drive, and open the Lesson08_Banner.fxp file.

2 Choose File > Import > Video/Sound File.

   The Import dialog box opens.

3 Browse to the Lesson08 folder on your hard drive. Ctrl/Command-click to select cityscape.flv, restaurants.flv, and button_click.mp3.

4 Click Open.

5 Open the Library panel and expand the Media category.

   The video and sound files you imported appear in the Library panel.

Preview video and sound

If your video and sound files have similar names, such as video1, video2, and so on, you can quickly identify them by previewing media in the Library panel. It's a good idea to preview media files before adding them to the application.

1 Select cityscape.flv in the Library panel.

   A still image appears at the top of the Library panel. The image includes a Play button. If you play the video, Rewind and Pause buttons appear.

Play button

Rewind and Pause buttons

2 Preview the cityscape.flv and restaurants.flv video files.

3 Select the button_click.mp3 sound file in the Library panel.

A Play button appears at the top of the Library panel. If you play the sound, Rewind and Pause buttons appear.

Play button   Rewind and Pause buttons

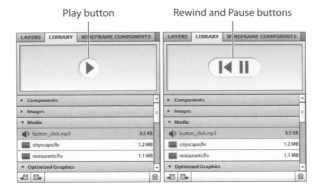

4 Preview the button_click.mp3 sound file.

It sounds like a button click.

Adding video to an application

There are two ways to add video to the application.

- Import a single video file directly into the current state.

- Drag a video from the Library panel to the artboard in the current state.

When you add a video to the application, the source video is stored in the library and a Video Player object is added to the current state and appears in the Layers panel. The Video Player is a container used to hold and play the video.

Add video to the artboard

The interactive banner application includes a custom component called Image Slider. The Image Slider component includes background images for each page. You are going to replace the background image for the Restaurants page with a short video clip.

1 Select the Restaurants page in the Pages/States panel.

2 Collapse the Timelines panel so you can see more of the artboard. If you can't see the entire artboard in the workspace, then change the workspace magnification to 66%.

3 In the Layers panel, unlock the Image Slider row.

4 In the artboard, double-click the background image to edit the Image Slider component in Edit-In-Place mode.

5 In the Layers panel, select Restaurants Image and click the Delete icon (🗑) in the Layers panel to remove it from all states in the application.

Removing the still image leaves a gap in the Image Slider. You'll fill the gap with the restaurants.flv video.

● **Note:** The Image Slider component is named Image Slider in the Layers panel, but its component name in the library is CustomComponent1. When you open the Image Slider component in Edit-In-Place mode, the name CustomComponent1 appears in the Breadcrumbs bar.

6 Open the Library panel and expand the Media category.

7 Drag a copy of the restaurants.flv video to the artboard and position it in the gap you created in step 5.

The video includes wireframe video controls below the video in the artboard. The video controls extend below the artboard, but that's OK because you're going to replace these with a custom control.

8 Open the Layers panel.

A Video Player object is added to the Layers panel in the Image Slider component.

Set video player properties

As with other objects, a video player can exist in more than one state, and it can have a unique set of properties in each state where it exists. You modify Video Player properties in the Properties panel.

1 Open the Common section in the Properties panel.

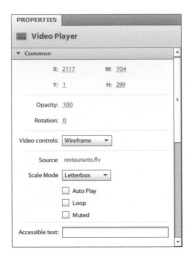

▶ **Tip:** Using the same video player to load and control different videos in different states is one way to optimize the performance of your application.

You can set the position, size, opacity, and rotation of the video. By default, the wireframe video controls are added below the video. To change which video appears in the controller, you can use the Source link in the Properties panel. This allows you to update the video without going through the steps to add, position, and set properties all over again. The properties apply to the Video Player, not the video file it contains.

2 Open the Video Controls menu and choose Standard.

The controls below the video player change from the blue wireframe controls to a standard set of black and white controls.

3 Open the Scale Mode pop-up menu and choose Letterbox. This should be the default setting. Scale Mode controls how the video scales when you drag its selection handles.

None sizes the video player but not the video picture. If you make the bounding box smaller than the video, the video is cropped.

Letterbox scales uniformly as large as possible without cropping the video. Black or white bars appear around the video if the video is a different aspect ratio than the video player bounding box.

Stretch matches the size of the video picture to the size of the video player window. This does not maintain its height to width ratio. The video is not cropped, but can appear distorted from the non-uniform scaling.

Zoom sizes and crops the video to match the size of the video player while maintaining the video's height to width ratio.

In the Properties panel, you can set the video to begin playing automatically (Auto Play), loop repeatedly (Loop), or begin with its sound muted (Muted).

You can enter Accessible text, which is recognized by screen readers and other accessibility programs.

4 Open the Component section of the Properties panel.

If the video includes sound, you can adjust its volume. You can also create a tooltip for the video player.

5 Open the Text section in the Properties panel, click the Color swatch and select a new color, such as red.

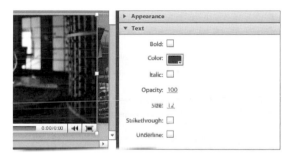

The text in the video controls change to the color you selected. You can also change the style, opacity, and size of the text.

6 In the Common section of the Properties panel, open the Video Controls menu and choose None.

This removes the video controls below the video player. You're going to replace these with a custom play/pause button.

> **Tip:** You can add filters to a video player in the Filters section of the Properties panel. For example, you can use a drop shadow to make it look like the video is floating above the artboard. You'll learn more about applying filters later in this course.

7 Press Esc to exit Edit-In-Place mode.

Controlling video playback

Now that you've hidden the default video controls, you need to give the user another way of playing and stopping the video in the Restaurants page.

You can use original artwork to create a custom video controller component. The controller can be as simple as a button used to play the video, or it can be a complex custom component that contains separate controls for things like play, pause, rewind, and so on.

Once you define the parts of your controller, you need to add interactions to control video playback. A control can be created from any component or group.

Attach controls to the video

The interactive banner application includes a Play/Pause toggle button that was created earlier. We can use this button to control the video, but the button and the video need to exist together, either at the main application level, or together inside the same component. Right now, the video player containing the restaurants video is located inside the Image Slider component, so we need to add the Toggle Button to the Image Slider.

1   Select the Restaurants page in the Pages/States panel, if it's not already selected.

2   In the Layers panel, unlock the Toggle Button row.

    You are going to move the Toggle Button into the Image Slider component, but to do this it needs to be unlocked.

3   Select Image Slider in the Layers panel, and click State1 in the Heads-Up Display (HUD) to edit the component in Edit-In-Place mode.

4   In the Layers panel, expand the Lesson08_Banner section. Drag the Toggle Button from the Lesson08_Banner section into the Image Slider component (CustomComponent1). Position the Toggle Button as the topmost layer.

    A message warns you that if you move the Toggle Button, you will lose any effects or interactions that are applied to it. This includes transitions and action sequences. If you want to use the Toggle Button component to control the video inside the Image Slider, you need to place the button inside the Image Slider component.

5   Click OK.

    The Toggle Button is the top layer in the Image Slider component.

    ● **Note:** You could have deleted the Toggle Button in the main application layers, and then dragged a new instance of the Toggle Button from the Library panel into the Image Slider custom component. But dragging the button from the main application into the component is faster.

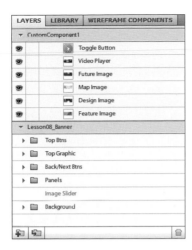

6 In the Layers panel, select Toggle Button, hold down Shift, and select Video Player.

Both objects are selected in the artboard.

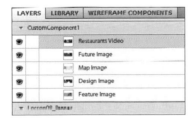

7 In the HUD, convert the selected objects to a Custom/Generic component.

8 In the Layers panel, rename the new custom component **Restaurants Video**.

9 In the HUD, click State1 to edit the Restaurants Video component in Edit-In-Place mode.

This component includes the Toggle Button and Video Player. With both objects inside the same component, you can use the Toggle Button to control the Video Player.

You can tell by the Layers panel that you're editing a custom component (CustomComponent2) that is located inside another custom component (CustomComponent1), which is located in the Lesson08_Banner application.

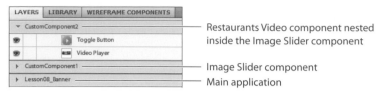 — Restaurants Video component nested inside the Image Slider component
— Image Slider component
— Main application

10 Click Duplicate State in the Pages/States panel.

11 Rename State1 **VideoPaused** and State2 **VideoPlaying**.

Having two states makes it possible to change the appearance of the button while the video is playing.

12 Make sure VideoPlaying is selected in the Pages/States panel.

13 Select Toggle Button in the Layers panel.

14 Change the Opacity value of the Toggle Button to **50** in the Properties panel.

When the video is playing (in the VideoPlaying state), the Toggle Button dims to 50% opacity.

15 In the Timelines panel, select VideoPaused > VideoPlaying in the State Transitions list.

16 Click Smooth Transition.

The Toggle Button begins at 100% opacity in the VideoPaused state and fades out to 50% opacity in the VideoPlaying state, creating a smooth transition. You can preview this by clicking the Play Transition button in the Timeline.

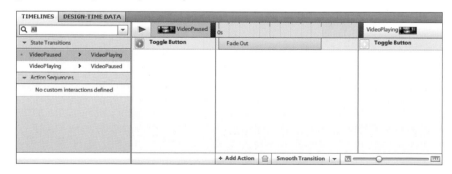

▶ **Tip:** If you want the Toggle Button to be invisible (not just dimmed) when the video is playing, you can edit the Toggle Button so that no artwork is visible in its Selected Up state or change its opacity value to 0.

17 Collapse the Timelines panel.

Add interactions to control video playback

With the Video Player and the Toggle Button together in the same component, the Toggle Button can now control the video.

1 Select the Toggle Button.

2 In the Interactions panel, add the following four On Click interactions:

- Play Video, Video Player – restaurants.flv, When In VideoPaused.

- Play Transition To State, VideoPlaying, When In VideoPaused.

- Pause Video, Video Player – restaurants.flv, When In VideoPlaying.

- Play Transition To State, VideoPaused, When In VideoPlaying.

The Toggle Button now includes four On Click interactions.

3 Run the project in a browser, navigate to the Restaurants page (page 4), and test the video controls.

Notice that when the video finishes playing, the Toggle Button remains at 50% opacity and doesn't toggle back to the play symbol. There are two problems. The Restaurants Video component is ending in the VideoPlaying state, and the Toggle Button stays selected (pause symbol). It should toggle back to its deselected Up state (play symbol). You'll fix that next.

4 Close the browser and return to Flash Catalyst.

The Restaurants Video component is still in edit in Edit-In-Place mode.

Reset the video after playing

To reset the video and Toggle Button after playing, you must do two things:

- Add an interaction that returns the Restaurants Video component to its VideoPaused state.

- Sync the Toggle Button so that its properties in each state match its natural on/off behavior, allowing it to toggle to the correct setting when returning to the VideoPaused state.

Tip: The clickable area of a button is defined by its boundaries. To enlarge the clickable area of a button, you can add a shape that's larger than the button. Place the shape in a new layer inside the button component, and change the shape's opacity value to 0.

1 Select Video Player in the Layers panel.

2 In the Interactions panel, click Add Interaction.

On Video Play Complete is the event that will trigger the interaction. This is the only option available because you have a video player selected. Play Transition To State is selected by default, and that's what you want.

3 Click Choose State, and select VideoPaused.

4 Click OK.

The Video Player will return to the VideoPaused state when the video is finished playing.

5 Select VideoPaused in the Pages/States panel.

6 Select the Toggle Button, and look in the Common section of the Properties panel.

By default, the Toggle Button is not selected. This is perfect because the Toggle Button begins in the VideoPaused state and is not selected until someone clicks it.

7 Double-click the Toggle Button to view its states in Edit-In-Place mode.

The Toggle Button begins deselected with its Up state (play symbol) visible. When someone clicks the button, it changes to its Selected Up state (pause symbol).

8 Press Esc to close the Toggle Button.

9 Select VideoPlaying in the Pages/States panel, select the Toggle Button, and look in the Properties panel.

When the video is playing (after the button is clicked), the button toggles to its Selected Up state but its properties are telling us that it's not selected. This causes a conflict, and the button loses sync because the button property doesn't reflect that it is selected while playing. To fix that, we need to change the button's Selected property to match its Selected Up state when the video is playing.

10 In the Properties panel for the Toggle Button, click the Selected property to select it.

11 Run the project in a browser, navigate to the Restaurants page (page 4), and test the video controls.

Now when the video finishes playing, it automatically returns to the VideoPaused state and the button toggles to the play symbol.

12 Close the browser and return to Flash Catalyst.

13 Click Lesson08_Banner in the Breadcrumbs bar to exit Edit-In-Place mode.

14 Lock the Image Slider layer in the Layers panel.

Adding sound effects

Sound effects aren't just fun. They improve usability by identifying buttons, menus, and other interactive objects.

You can add sound effects to components or groups by adding an action sequence interaction and then adding a Sound Effect to the action sequence in the Timelines panel.

1 Unlock the Top Btns layer in the Layers panel, and open the Timelines panel.

The Top Btns layer includes the top five navigation buttons. You can add sound effects that play when someone clicks a button.

2 In the artboard, click to select the top navigation button labeled 1.

3 In the Interactions panel, click Add Interaction.

4 Choose On Roll Over, Play Action Sequence, and When In Any State.

5 Click OK.

An empty On Button Roll Over action sequence is added to the Timelines panel.

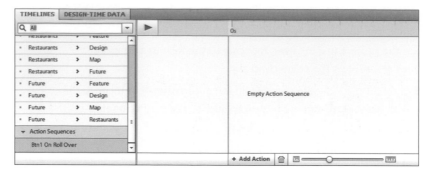

6 Click Add Action, and choose Sound Effect.

The Select Asset dialog box opens. You can add a sound from the Media category in the library or import a new sound.

7 Click Import.

The Import dialog box opens to the Adobe Flash Catalyst CS5 sound effects directory.

● **Note:** If, when importing a sound effect from the Select Asset dialog box, your sound effects library does not include the Flash Beep.mp3 file, there is a copy of this file in the Lesson08/ xtra-sound folder on your hard drive. You can browse to this file, select it, and click Open.

8 Select the Flash Beep.mp3 file, and click Open.

The Flash Beep.mp3 file is added to the Media category in the library and is selected in the Select Asset dialog box.

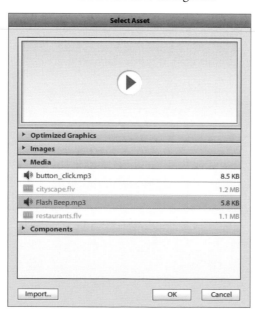

9 Click the Play button at the top of the Select Asset dialog box to preview the Flash Beep.mp3 file.

10 Click OK to add the sound effect.

The Flash Beep.mp3 sound effect is added to the action sequence.

Play button   Rewind handle

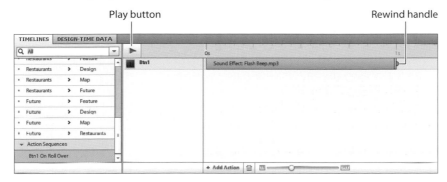

11 Click the Play button in the Timelines panel to preview the action sequence.

The sound effect plays.

The duration of the sound effect is 1 second. If the sound was longer than 1 second, you would need to extend its duration to match the length of the audio file. You can do that in the Properties panel or by dragging its resize handle.

The sound plays immediately when the interaction occurs.

12 In the Properties panel, select the Repeat property.

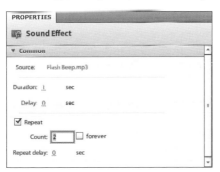

The Repeat property expands. You can enter the number of times you want the sound effect to repeat, or choose Forever if you want the sound effect to continue playing without stopping.

13 Click the Play button in the Timelines panel.

The sound effect plays the number of times entered in the Properties panel.

14 Deselect Repeat so the sound effect plays once when someone rolls over the navigation button.

> **Tip:** You can delay the start of the sound by dragging the Sound Effect bar in the Timeline, or by changing its Delay property in the Properties panel.

> **Tip:** When repeating a sound effect, you can set a Repeat Delay value. Repeat Delay creates a pause between each repetition of the sound effect. For example, if you have a sound effect of a heartbeat, you can repeat it and use the Repeat Delay value to control the audible heart rate.

15 Add another action sequence to the top navigation button labeled 1, but this time make it an On Click interaction that plays the button_click.mp3 sound effect that you imported to the library.

The top navigation button labeled 1 includes three interactions. The first is the On Click interaction that navigates to the Feature page (page 1). A second On Click action sequence plays the button_click.mp3 sound effect. The On Roll Over action sequence plays the Flash Beep.mp3 sound effect.

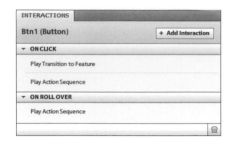

16 Run the project in a browser and click back and forth between the first and second pages to test the sound effects.

Notice that when you're on page 1, the Top Btn 1 sound effects don't play. That's because the button is disabled in its target state.

▶ **Tip:** To associate a sound effect with a transition, add the sound effect to the object that triggers the transition.

17 Close the browser and return to Flash Catalyst.

18 Add the same On Roll Over and On Click sound effects to the other top navigation buttons.

Using an audio-only FLV

One way to gain greater control over the playback of sound is to import an "audio-only" FLV file. This is a video file with an audio track, but no video. When you add an audio-only FLV file to your project, the file is contained in a video player. You get all the same properties and controls that you have when adding a video.

Audio-only FLV files are helpful when you want to include an audio track, such as narration or background music, and then control the playback of that file using wireframe, standard, or custom video controls.

Review questions

1 How can you import a video file directly to the artboard for the current state in the application (without dragging it from the Library panel)?

2 How do you set a video to play continuously?

3 How can I set a video to begin playing automatically, without requiring someone to click a Play button?

4 By default, what is used to control the playback of video?

5 What rule applies when using a component to control video playback?

6 What types of objects can include sound effects?

7 How do you add a sound effect to a component or group?

Review answers

1 If you import one video at a time, the video is added to the current state. Importing multiple videos places them in the library only.

2 Select the video player and select Loop in the Properties panel to play a video continuously.

3 Select the video player and select Auto Play in the Properties panel to play a video automatically.

4 By default, the wireframe video controls are added below the video in the video player. In the video player Properties panel, you can change to the standard controls, or hide the controls by choosing None, and then create custom controls using other components.

5 The component and the video player must both be in the main application layers or together inside the same component. For example, a component in the main application layers cannot be used to control a video that is nested inside other components.

6 You can attach sound effects to components and groups.

7 To add a sound effect, select the component or group. Add an action sequence to the component or group. In the Timelines panel, open the Add Action menu and add a Sound Effect.

9 INTEGRATING SWF CONTENT FROM OTHER CREATIVE SUITE TOOLS

Lesson Overview

When it comes to effective visual communication, keeping the attention of your audience is a challenge. Designing engaging and meaningful content requires thinking outside the box and leveraging a wide range of design tools, including vector-based animation, with a purpose—to tell a story, explain a concept, demonstrate a procedure, or simply entertain.

Flash Catalyst does an excellent job with smooth transitions using simple fades and movement. You can also produce more elaborate animation using other Adobe Creative Suite tools and then publish your movie as a SWF file. The SWF file is imported as an asset in your Flash Catalyst project.

In this lesson, you'll learn how to do the following:

- Use SWF files in Flash Catalyst projects

- Add SWF files to an application

- Control the playback of a SWF file

- Play a SWF file from a specific frame

- Create an animated button using a SWF file

 This lesson will take about 40 minutes to complete. Copy the Lesson09 folder into the lessons folder that you created on your hard drive for these projects (or create it now), if you haven't already done so. As you work on this lesson, you won't be preserving the start files; if you need to restore the start files, copy them from the *Adobe Flash Catalyst CS5 Classroom in a Book* CD.

Quickly extend the capabilities of your Flash Catalyst project by importing complex interactive animation and movies published in the SWF file format. Add immersive content or interactive video created in Adobe Flash Professional to create a more compelling user experience.

SWF files

SWF, pronounced *swif*, is short for Shockwave Flash and is the dominant format for displaying animated vector graphics and text, as well as sound and video, over the Internet. The SWF file format delivers vector graphics, text, video, and sound and is viewed using Adobe Flash Player and Adobe AIR software. Flash Player reaches over 98 percent of Internet-enabled desktops and more than 800 million hand helds and mobile devices.

Creating SWF files for Flash Catalyst

Browse the web and you'll find page after page of computer programs for publishing your finished web content in the SWF file format. These include several Adobe Creative Suite applications and a long list of third-party programs.

You can use the following Adobe applications to output SWF files:

- Adobe Flash Professional CS4 or CS5 (recommended for Flash Catalyst SWF content)
- Adobe Premiere Pro
- Adobe After Effects
- Adobe Encore
- Adobe Fireworks
- Adobe InDesign
- Adobe Illustrator
- Adobe Media Encoder
- Adobe Captivate*
- Adobe Presenter*

● **Note:** * Indicates an application that is not part of Adobe Creative Suite.

Searchable SWF content

A common complaint when using SWF content is that it's virtually impossible to locate using today's search engines. But that's all changing.

Adobe is working with Google and Yahoo to enable one of the largest fundamental improvements in web search results by making the Flash file format (SWF) a first-class citizen in searchable web content. This will enable top search engines to locate the content you've embedded inside the rich Internet applications you build using Flash Catalyst. This will also provide more relevant automatic search rankings of the millions of RIAs and other dynamic content that run in Adobe Flash Player.

Using SWF files in Flash Catalyst

With so many applications capable of outputting SWF content, there's a lot of potential to leverage existing materials in your rich Internet applications. However, it's important to know that not all SWF content is created equal. Take a few minutes to review the following tips before acquiring SWF content for use in your Flash Catalyst projects:

- **Controlling the playback of SWF content in Flash Catalyst.** You can add Flash Catalyst effects in the Timelines panel to control the playback of a SWF file. Only SWF content written in ActionScript 3.0 and published using Adobe Flash Professional can be controlled using Flash Catalyst effects.

- **Importing Flash Professional SWF content.** You can import SWF files created in Flash Professional into Flash Catalyst, but there is no direct integration between the two applications. If you need to edit the SWF file, make your changes in Flash Professional, republish, and import the new file into Flash Catalyst. Then, select the SWF Asset in your application and use the Source link in the Properties panel to swap the old SWF file for the new one you've added to the library.

- **Loading content dynamically.** Many SWF files are complex interactive applications that load content dynamically at runtime. For example, a movie.swf file may include a link to video stored externally in a folder named My Video. You can import the movie.swf file into Flash Catalyst, but you'll need to manually copy the source video to your published Flash Catalyst project folders. The linked video must maintain the same position relative to Main.swf that it had relative to movie.swf. For example, if the video is stored in the My Video folder next to movie.swf, then copy the My Video folder and paste it next to the Main.swf file that's created when you publish your Flash Catalyst project. If you publish more than one version of the application (for example, web, offline, AIR), you'll need to manually copy the video to all locations.

The movie.swf file is imported into Flash Catalyst.

In the Flash Catalyst project directory, the SWF file resides in assets/images, so you might think the video goes here too.

It will only work if the video goes here.

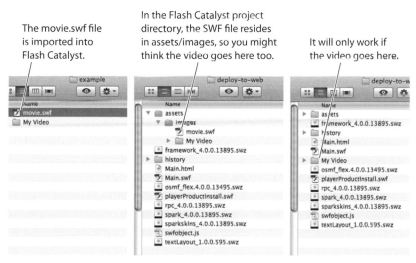

Tip: If you publish lots of SWF content that includes TLF text, you can save a custom publish profile for repeated use. To save a publish profile, select your preferred settings and click the Create New Profile button (+) in the Publish Settings dialog box. Enter a name for the profile and click OK.

- **Merging a shared library.** Flash Professional CS5 includes two types of text—Text Layout Framework (TLF) and Classic. TLF was introduced with Flash Professional CS4 and is the new default way to create text in Flash Professional. TLF text delivers multilingual, print-quality typography for the web and offers formatting not possible with Classic text. When publishing SWF files that include TLF text, the Flash Professional CS5 default is to generate two files, a SWF file and a SWZ file. The SWZ file is a text layout library. You must merge the shared library into the underlying code of the SWF file before you can use the SWF file in Flash Catalyst.

To merge a shared library in Flash Professional CS4:

1. In Flash Professional CS5, choose File > Publish Settings and select the Flash tab.

2. On the Flash tab, click the Script: ActionScript 3.0 Settings button and select the Library Path tab.

3. On the Library Path tab, in the Runtime Shared Library Settings section, select Merged Into Code from the Default Linkage pop-up menu.

4. Publish the SWF file.

Tip: There is a lot of really good, royalty-free SWF content available that can be a great addition to your Flash Catalyst projects.

Use ActionScript 3.0 for SWF content used in Flash Catalyst

ActionScript is the powerful object-oriented programming language behind the scenes of every SWF file. When you create and publish a SWF file using Adobe Flash Professional, you choose which version of ActionScript to use. Any content you plan to import to Flash Catalyst should be written and published using ActionScript 3.0.

Adding SWF files to Flash Catalyst

Note: If you import more than one SWF file at the same time, the files are added to the project library, but no assets are added to the artboard until you drag them from the Library panel.

When you import a SWF file into Flash Catalyst, it's stored as an asset in the Images category of the project library. An instance of the SWF file is added to the current state automatically. You can share that same instance of the SWF file to other states just like you can with images, video, and other objects. Once you've imported the SWF file to the library, you can use it anywhere in your application by dragging it from the Library panel to the artboard.

Tip: Remember that each time you drag a SWF file from the Library panel to the artboard, you are creating another instance of the asset in your application. If you want the SWF file to appear in more than one state, then add one instance and then share that same instance to the other states.

Import a SWF file to the artboard

Let's add the animated logo for the Restaurant Guide application. The logo is a SWF file that we can import directly to the artboard.

1 Start Flash Catalyst, browse to the Lesson09 folder on your hard drive, and open the Lesson09_Restaurants.fxp file.

This file is an interactive restaurant guide. An animated logo belongs at the top of the page. The logo was created and published as a SWF file.

2 Select the Home page in the Pages/States panel.

3 Choose File > Import > SWF File.

4 Browse to the Lesson09 folder on your hard drive, select logo_wave.swf, and click Open.

The SWF movie appears in the artboard on the Home page and the SWF Asset appears in the Layers panel.

5 In the artboard, drag the animated logo (SWF Asset) to position it in the empty space at the top of the page.

The first frame of the SWF movie is visible in the artboard. The entire content of this SWF file is located in Frame 1 of the movie, including the animated flag, so you don't need to play the movie to see it.

6 Make sure the SWF file is selected, and choose States > Share To State > SubPages.

The SWF file is added to the top of the SubPages state.

Preview a SWF animation

You can't preview a SWF movie in the Flash Catalyst Library panel the way you can a video or still image, but you *can* preview the movie by running the project.

1   Open the Library panel.

2   Expand the Images category and select the logo_wave.swf file.

The SWF icon appears in the preview window in the Library panel.

3   Run the project in a browser.

In a browser, you can see the SWF movie. In this case it looks just like it did in Flash Catalyst, because the entire contents of the movie are occurring in a single frame.

4   Close the browser and return to Flash Catalyst.

5   Close the Lesson09_Restaurants.fxp files, without saving changes, and keep Flash Catalyst open.

Controlling the playback of SWF files

Most SWF files consist of more than one frame, and many involve internal navigation or other interactivity. For these SWF files, you'll need to add an interaction that tells the movie when to play or stop. You can even tell the SWF file to begin playing or stop on a specific frame within the movie.

Play or stop a SWF file

To play or stop a SWF file, add an interaction that triggers an action sequence when someone clicks or rolls over a component or group, or when the application starts. In the action sequence, add an effect to control the playback of the SWF file.

To see how this works, let's add an On Application Start interaction that plays a SWF file automatically when someone opens the application.

1 Open the Lesson09_Photo_Traveler.fxp file. It's located in the Lesson09 folder on your hard drive.

2 Choose File > Import > SWF File. Browse to the Lesson09 folder, select the traveler.swf file, and click Open.

A new SWF Asset is added to the top of the artboard and appears in the Layers panel, inside the SWF folder. You may need to expand the SWF folder to see the SWF Asset in the Layers panel.

3 Choose Modify > Align > Bottom to position the SWF Asset at the bottom of the artboard.

This SWF file begins transparent in Frame 1 and fades into view during the first 20 frames of the movie, so you don't see much in the artboard.

4 Choose Edit > Deselect All to make sure nothing is selected in the artboard.

5 In the Interactions panel, click Add Interaction.

Because nothing is selected in the artboard, the interaction defaults to On Application Start.

6 Choose Play Action Sequence as the interaction type.

7 Click OK.

The new On Application Start action sequence is selected in the Timelines panel.

8 In the Layers panel, expand the SWF folder and click SWF Asset to select the SWF file in the artboard.

9 In the Timelines panel, click Add Action and choose SWF Control > Play - play().

A Play SWF effect is added to the On Application Start action sequence in the Timeline.

Play SWF effect

10 Run the project in a browser.

The SWF movie begins playing as soon as the application starts.

The application links at the top of the window aren't connected to any pages yet, but you can test the SWF file by clicking its right and left arrow keys.

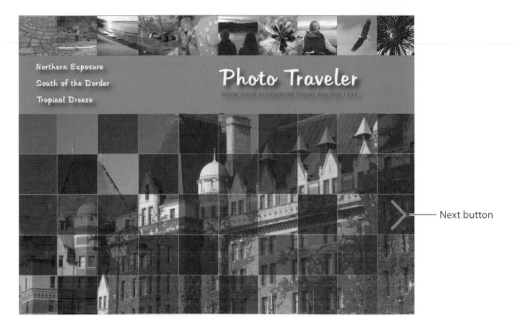

Next button

11 Explore the SWF movie by clicking the Next button (right arrow) twice. When you're finished exploring, close the browser and return to Flash Catalyst.

Play the SWF movie from a specific frame

You can tell the movie to begin playing on a specific frame in the SWF file's main timeline. This allows you to build controls in Flash Catalyst that go to and play or stop at different locations within the SWF movie.

1 Select the Play SWF effect in the Timelines panel.

2 In the Timelines panel, click the Delete icon (🗑) to delete the effect.

Deleting the effect does not remove the action sequence, only the effect. The On Application Start action sequence is still selected in the Timelines panel.

3 Click Add Action and choose SWF Control > Go To Frame And Play - gotoAndPlay().

The Go To Frame And Play effect appears in the Timeline.

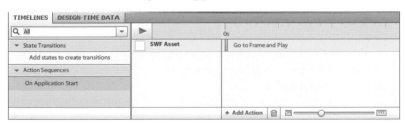

Note: In this activity you use a Go To Frame And Play effect to begin a movie at Frame 31, but why Frame 31? This is a starting point of another section in the movie, but you can just as easily go to any other frame. Having knowledge of the SWF file's main timeline will help determine which frame to use in a Go To Frame And Play (or Stop) effect.

4 In the Properties panel, change the Start Frame value to **31**.

This tells the action sequence to begin playing the SWF movie at Frame 31 of its main timeline.

5 Run the project in a browser.

This time when the application starts, the SWF movie plays automatically, but it begins on Frame 31.

6 Close the Lesson09_Photo_Traveler.fxp file without saving changes, but leave Flash Catalyst open.

Adding a SWF file to a component

You can use an imported SWF file to bring buttons and other components to life by using creative animation techniques that aren't available in the current Flash Catalyst collection of effects.

To illustrate this, let's add some animation to a sample button. We've already created a simple animated SWF file of two gears rotating in opposite directions. This will be a nice complement to our button.

Tip: You can add Go To Frame And Play or Go To Frame And Stop interactions to navigation buttons that you create in Flash Catalyst, and then use the different buttons to quickly begin playing or go to and stop a SWF movie at various locations.

Position a SWF file

First, you need to position the SWF file on the sample button.

1   Open the Lesson09_Animated_Button file. It's located in the Lesson09 folder on your hard drive.

    The file includes a navigation button that's partially designed. To complete the button, you will add a SWF animation.

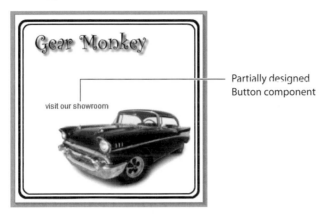

Partially designed
Button component

2   In the Layers panel, select the Button object. In the Heads-Up Display (HUD), click Up to edit the button in Edit-In-Place mode.

    The button opens with the Up state selected.

3   Import the gear_button.swf file. It's located in the Lesson09 folder.

    The SWF Asset is added as a new object in the Button component layers.

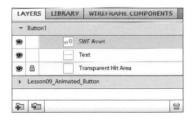

4   In the artboard, position the gear_button SWF file so that it's centered above the text in the Button component.

5   With the button selected in the Up state, choose States > Share To State > All States to copy the SWF file to the Over, Down, and Disabled states.

Add effects to play the animation

With the SWF Asset in all states of the button, you can use transition effects to control when the animation is playing or stopped.

1 In the Timelines panel, select the Up > Over transition.

2 Select the SWF Asset in the artboard, if it's not already selected.

3 In the Timelines panel, choose Add Action > SWF Controls > Play - play().

The play effect is added to the transition between the Up and Over states of the button.

4 Select the Over > Up transition.

5 Choose Add Action > SWF Controls > Stop - stop().

The stop effect is added to the Over > Up transition.

6 Press Esc to exit Edit-In-Place mode.

7 Run the project in a browser and test the button.

When you roll over the button, the SWF animation plays and the gears appear to spin in opposite directions. When you move the pointer away from the button, the animation stops.

8 Close the browser and return to Flash Catalyst.

9 Close the Lesson09_Animated_Button file without saving changes.

Review questions

1 What is the recommended application for creating SWF content for use in Flash Catalyst projects?

2 What types of SWF files can be controlled using interactions in Flash Catalyst?

3 Does Flash Catalyst support SWF files that include links to external data, such as video that loads at runtime?

4 If a SWF file includes Text Layout Framework (TLF) text, what must be done to the file before it will play correctly in Flash Catalyst?

5 How do you preview a SWF file?

6 When does a SWF file play automatically without adding any type of interaction or transition effects in Flash Catalyst?

7 What are two ways to add play or stop controls to a SWF file in Flash Catalyst?

Review answers

1 The recommended application for creating Flash Content is Adobe Flash Professional CS4 or CS5.

2 Only SWF content written in ActionScript 3.0 and published using Adobe Flash Professional can be controlled in Flash Catalyst.

3 Flash Catalyst supports SWF files with links to external files, but the linked content must maintain its original position relative to the SWF file being imported. If you publish more than one version of the application, you'll need to manually copy the linked content to all locations in the published directories.

4 Flash Professional includes two types of text: Text Layout Framework (TLF) and Classic. When publishing SWF files that include TLF text, Flash Professional's default is to generate two files, a SWF file and a SWZ file. The SWZ file is a text layout library. You must merge the shared library into the underlying code of the SWF file before you can use the SWF file in Flash Catalyst.

5 To preview a SWF file, you must run the project in a browser or publish the project. You cannot preview a SWF file in the Library or Timelines panels.

6 If the entire SWF movie occurs in the first frame of its internal main timeline, the SWF file plays without adding controls in Flash Catalyst.

7 You can control a SWF file in Flash Catalyst by using an action sequence with a SWF Control effect. You can also add the SWF file to the Up and Over states in a Button component and then add a SWF Control effect to the transitions between states.

10 DESIGNING WITH DATA

Lesson Overview

What do you get when you combine Flash Catalyst's visual interface design functionality with its design-time data feature for building pixel-perfect models of data-centric applications? As a designer, you get the flexibility to rapidly generate data-driven interface components with both style and substance. You also maintain complete control over the look and feel of your final application, even after you hand it off to developers for integration with data servers and services.

In this lesson, you'll learn how to do the following:

- Design visually interesting interface components for browsing and displaying large collections of data

- Create a Data List component using images and text

- Set data list properties

- Use design-time data to demonstrate the appearance and behavior of a data list

- Add a wireframe Data List component

 This lesson will take about 60 minutes to complete. Copy the Lesson10 folder into the lessons folder that you created on your hard drive for these projects (or create it now), if you haven't already done so. As you work on this lesson, you won't be preserving the start files; if you need to restore the start files, copy them from the *Adobe Flash Catalyst CS5 Classroom in a Book* CD.

TIMELINES | DESIGN-TIME DATA

	Image 3	Image 10	Text 1	Text 2
0		★★★★★	This is one rowdy place! Bring your earplugs.	Phil
1		★★★★☆	Who doesn't like an all-you-can-drink-beer ...	K.W.
2		★★★☆☆		
3		★★☆☆☆		
4		★☆☆☆☆		
5		☆☆☆☆☆		
6		★☆☆☆☆		

REVIEWS　　POST REVIEW　　VIEW STATS

Phil　★★★★★

This is one rowdy place! Bring your earplugs.

K.W.　★★★★☆

Who doesn't like an all-you-can-drink-beer keg???

Collaborate more effectively with developers by providing them with fully designed data-centric user interface components that can be extended using Adobe Flash Builder to add functionality and integration with servers and services.

Flash Catalyst data lists

A data list is a special type of component used to retrieve and display a series of related items. You can design a data list using Flash Catalyst. Typically, you'll include enough sample records to demonstrate the layout and behavior of the list. Once you finalize the look and feel, a Flex developer can use Adobe Flash Builder to connect your Data List component to a web service that retrieves and displays any number of records when the application runs.

A list is not always a list

The name data *list* is a little misleading. Each unique record in a Flash Catalyst data list can include artwork, text, or a combination of both. It doesn't need to be a list at all. Traditionally, a data list might look something like a spreadsheet or data table.

Using Flash Catalyst, you can build a Data List component that displays a tiled wall of images.

A list can be a scrolling filmstrip or series of thumbnails, from which you select and view other content or navigate to new locations in the application. By adding a scroll bar, you can extend the list to include any number of items.

Of course, there's nothing stopping you from making your data list look like an ordinary list if that's what you want. In fact, there's even a built-in wireframe Data List component.

By default, the records in a data list can have different Normal, Over, and Selected states. You can use the Over state to reveal more information about a record when a user rolls over an item.

Normal state   Over state

What is design-time data?

When developing an application that's used to present large amounts of data, it's not always possible to see the end result until the application is running and connected to a back-end data source. That is unless you're using a Flash Catalyst Data List component and design-time data. Design-time data allows you to use *dummy* content, such as sample database records or bitmap images, without having to actually connect to a back-end system. This gives you, the designer, complete control over the final look and feel of the user experience. This also makes it possible for a developer using Adobe Flash Builder to replace the design-time data with real data from a database or web service while maintaining the interactions and pixel-perfect design from Flash Catalyst.

Preview a data list

Before you dive in and start making a new data list, let's take a moment to preview how a list appears when it's put together. Seeing a Data List component in action will help you to understand each of its parts and how they relate to one another in a working application.

1 Start Flash Catalyst. Browse to the Lesson10 folder on your hard drive and open the Restaurants_finished.fxp file.

2 Run the project in a browser.

When the application starts, it plays a short video and then stops on a horizontal list of restaurants. This is a horizontal data list. If you roll over an item in the list, you see its Over state. Scroll arrows let you move forward and backward through the list.

Data list items or records   Scroll arrow

3 Click the right scroll arrow to see more restaurants in the data list.

4 Click any restaurant.

Clicking an item in the data list takes you to a different page in the application. Each restaurant includes a Reviews button.

5 Click Reviews.

The restaurant reviews are included in a vertical data list. Each item in the list includes an image, the name of the reviewer, a short review, and a star rating.

6 Roll over and click a few of the reviews in the list.

The reviews have different Normal, Over, and Selected states. In the next exercise, you are going to re-create this data list.

7 Close the browser and return to Flash Catalyst.

8 Close the project without saving changes.

Creating a Data List component

There are three main steps to making a Data List component. These are:

- Design a sample item or record in the list. Add a scroll bar if your list will extend beyond the available space in the user interface.

- Convert the sample record (and scroll bar) into a Data List component.

- Define the elements that represent the repeated item (a single record).

Design a sample record

If you think about a traditional data list, there are typically columns and rows of information. Each row represents a unique record in the database. For each record there may be several columns of information. For example, an employee list displays each employee in a different row and includes columns for employee name, number, department, hire date, and so on.

In Flash Catalyst, records can be listed horizontally, vertically, or tiled. Each record can include text, numbers, images, and other artwork. The first step to making a Data List component is to pull together the elements that make up a single record. If your list requires a scroll bar, you can place it relative to the first item in the list.

1 Browse to the Lesson10 folder on your hard drive and open the Lesson10_
Restaurants.fxp file.

2 Select SubPages in the Pages/States panel.

3 In the Layers panel, select Sub Pages.

This selects the Sub Pages custom component in the artboard. The restaurant reviews data list will be nested inside the Info state in the Sub Pages custom component. Nesting components is an efficient way to create multiple views without adding additional application pages.

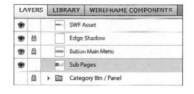

4 In the Heads-Up Display (HUD), click Info to edit the Sub Pages custom component in Edit-In-Place mode.

The component opens with the Info state selected. The Info state includes another nested component called Review Popup.

5 In the Layers panel, expand the Sub Pages layer folder, expand the Info layer folder, and select Review Popup.

The Review Popup custom component is selected in the artboard.

6 In the HUD, click Reviews to edit the Review Popup component in Edit-In-Place mode with the Reviews state selected.

This is where the restaurant reviews belong. This data list will include more reviews than can fit vertically in the Reviews Popup, so you'll need to add a vertical scroll bar.

7   In the Library panel, expand the Components category and select the Review_Popup_VerticalScrollbar component.

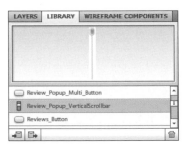

8   Drag the Review_Popup_VerticalScrollbar from the Library panel to the artboard. Position it along the right side of the empty white space.

Now let's import the artwork for a sample review that was designed in Adobe Photoshop.

9   Choose File > Import > Adobe Photoshop File (.psd). Browse to the Lesson10 folder, select the DataList_art.psd file, and click Open. Click OK to accept the default import fidelity options.

The sample review artwork is imported and selected in the artboard.

10 Position the artwork at the top of the reviews panel and to the left of the scroll bar.

You now have one sample record and a scroll bar.

Convert the sample record into a Data List component

With the parts of a data list arranged in the artboard, the next step is to select them and convert the individual parts into a new Data List component. If your data list includes a scroll bar, make sure to include it in the selection.

1 Make sure the artwork you imported in the previous task is still selected.

2 Hold down Shift and click the scroll bar to add it to the selection.

3 In the HUD, convert the artwork to a Data List component.

A message in the HUD informs you that to make the data list work correctly, you need to assign its parts. You need to tell it which parts to use as the repeated item.

Define the repeated item

Every Data List component must include a master item called the *repeated item*. The repeated item is a *template* that defines the appearance of every item or record in the list, including its Normal, Over, and Selected states.

Changes applied to the repeated item template are applied to every item in the list automatically at runtime. For example, if you change the opacity of an image in the Over state of the repeated item, this change applies to every record. Keep in mind that your application might display thousands of records. It's a huge time-saver and guarantees a consistent look across all records.

1   In the HUD, click Edit Parts to edit the data list in Edit-In-Place mode.

2   Select all five parts of the sample review record, including the round image, the line, the stars, and both lines of text. Do not select the scroll bar.

3   In the Convert To Data List Part section of the HUD, click Choose Part and select Repeated Item.

The artwork is turned into a repeated item. By default, the repeated item is arranged vertically in the data list. If it doesn't fit perfectly in the designed space, you can resize it. You'll do that next.

► **Tip:** When a component is in Edit-In-Place mode, you can drag to select its parts without selecting other objects in the artboard. You can also choose Edit > Select All and only objects in the component you're editing are selected.

Setting data list properties

The layout of a Data List component is determined mainly by its repeated item properties—size, position, orientation, spacing, and so on.

You can modify its properties in the artboard and by changing its values in the Properties panel.

Size and position the bounding box

The repeated item bounding box indicates the visible and scrollable area in the data list. You define this space by sizing the bounding box in the artboard or in the Properties panel.

1   Make sure the repeated item is still selected.

2   In the Common section of the Properties panel, change the height (H:) value to **500**.

The bounding box height adjusts. You can now see the five sample records that were added to the list automatically. You can also size the bounding box using its handles.

3 Use the handles to resize the bounding box height and width and position it to fit in the space designed for the reviews. The height of the box should be equal to the height of the vertical scroll bar.

Edit the repeated item layout

By default, the repeated item is aligned vertically. There is a small amount of space between each record in the list, and the artwork is positioned right up against the left, right, top, and bottom sides of the bounding box. This is called *padding*. You can change these settings in the Layout section of the Properties panel. You can also change the appearance of objects in the Normal, Over, and Selected states.

1 Make sure the repeated item is still selected.

2 Expand the Layout section of the Properties panel.

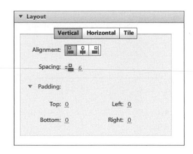

A repeated item has three possible layouts. These include Vertical, Horizontal, and Tile. The default setting is Vertical, and that's what you want for the restaurant reviews. You can also change the alignment of the list within the bounding box.

3 Change the Spacing value to **10**.

Spacing is the distance between each item in the list. *Padding* refers to the space between the list items and the bounding box.

4 Select the Horizontal layout option.

The items align horizontally.

▶ **Tip:** A data list has the same properties as every other Flash Catalyst built-in component. For example, you can change its size, opacity, and rotation. You can enable or disable it, add a tooltip, or add a drop shadow.

5 Select the Tile layout option.

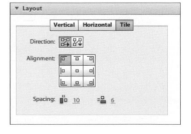

The Tile option is used to arrange a collection of images or text in a tiled mosaic pattern. You can adjust the direction and alignment of the tiles. You can also adjust the spacing between rows and columns in the mosaic.

6 Change back to the Vertical layout option.

Edit the repeated item states

Every repeated item begins with slightly different Normal, Over, and Selected states so that a user can see when they are rolling over or selecting an item in the list. You can edit the states of the repeated item template, just like you can with components.

1 Double-click the repeated item in the artboard to edit it in Edit-In-Place mode.

The Normal, Over, and Selected states appear in the Pages/States panel.

● **Note:** You cannot duplicate, add, or remove states in the repeated item, but you can modify the artwork that appears in each of the default states (Normal, Over, and Selected).

2 Select the Over state in the Pages/States panel and open the Layers panel.

The Over state includes the Item Highlight Rectangle to show when the pointer is over the item in the list.

3 Select Item Highlight Rectangle in the Layers panel.

4 In the Common section of the Properties panel, change the rectangle's fill color to pale green.

Notice, the rectangle's opacity is already set to 30, which makes it semi-transparent.

5 Run the project in a browser.

6 Click any of the restaurants in the horizontal list, and then click Reviews to see your new data list.

7 Use the scroll bar to see all five items in the list.

Right now every item has the same artwork. You are going to change that next using design-time data.

8 Roll over and select an item in the list to see the Normal, Over, and Selected states.

9 Close the browser and return to Flash Catalyst.

10 Click Review_Popup in the Breadcrumbs bar.

This closes the repeated item and the data list. The Review_Popup component is still in Edit-In-Place mode.

Using design-time data

▶ **Tip:** There is nothing stopping you from creating a finished data list using design-time data and images in the project library. You don't have to connect the application to an external data source. However, if your application is used to display large amounts of data that change over time, binding your list to external data is a better choice.

Most data lists are connected to a data source and populated with data dynamically at runtime. A developer can make this connection using Adobe Flash Builder. In Flash Catalyst, you can add placeholder data to display in the Data List component using the Design-Time Data panel. In fact, five sample records are created automatically when you first create the Data List component. Each sample record is a copy of the repeated item in the data list. Using the Design-Time Data panel, you can replace the sample repeated images and text with more realistic examples of the actual data that you want displayed. This dummy data is called design-time data.

It's a good idea to include a representative sample, so that your developer knows exactly how you want the data to appear in the finished application.

Replace design-time images

Replacing the repeated sample data is easy. Open the Design-Time Data panel and swap the images for new ones.

1 Select the Data List component in the Layers panel.

The data list is selected in the artboard. Using the Layers panel to select the data list is a good way to make sure you select only the data list and not the image below it.

2 Open the Design-Time Data panel and drag the top border of the panel to make it taller.

The Design-Time Data panel organizes sample data similarly to a traditional data table. Each record is listed as a separate row, and the information in each record (images and text) is listed in columns. In this list, each item includes three images (stars, a round image, and a line) and two pieces of text (the review and the reviewer's name). At first, the design-time data includes five copies of the repeated item, numbered from 0 to 4.

	Image 1	Image 2	Image 3	Text 1	Text 2
0	★★★★★			This is one rowdy place! Bring your earplugs.	Phil
1	★★★★★			This is one rowdy place! Bring your earplugs.	Phil
2	★★★★★			This is one rowdy place! Bring your earplugs.	Phil
3	★★★★★			This is one rowdy place! Bring your earplugs.	Phil
4	★★★★★			This is one rowdy place! Bring your earplugs.	Phil

TIMELINES DESIGN-TIME DATA

3   Click the round image (in the Image 2 column) in row number 1 (the second row). Be sure to select the image in row number 1, not row number 0.

The Select Asset dialog box appears. You can choose an image in the project library or choose Import to add another image.

4   Select reviewPopupIcon01.png and click OK.

The new image appears in the Design-Time Data panel.

5   Click the stars (in the Image 1 column) in row 1.

6   In the Select Asset dialog box, select reviewPopup4Stars.png and click OK.

The second review now has a four-star rating.

7 Replace the round image in row 2 with reviewPopupIcon02.png.

8 Replace the stars in row 2 with reviewPopup3Stars.png.

9 Replace the round image in row 3 with reviewPopupIcon03.png.

10 Replace the stars in row 3 with reviewPopup2Stars.png.

11 Replace the round image in row 4 with reviewPopupIcon04.png.

12 Replace the stars in row 4 with reviewPopup1Star.png.

The design-time data for the restaurant reviews data list now includes a more realistic collection of sample images.

▶ **Tip:** By default, a data list opens with nothing selected. You can set the list to open with a specific record selected. To do this, select a row in the Design-Time Data panel. Then in the Component section of the Properties panel, enter 1 as the value for the Selected Index property. The row you selected will display its Selected state when the application runs.

Edit design-time text

Replacing sample design-time text is even easier than swapping images. Open the Design-Time Data panel, and enter new text for each record.

1 In the Design-Time Data panel, click in the Text 1 column for row 1 and type a new review.

▶ **Tip:** You can press the Tab key to quickly move between text fields in the Design-Time Data panel.

2 Click in the Text 2 column for row 1 and type a new reviewer name.

3 Add new reviews and reviewer names for the design-time data in rows 2, 3, and 4.

4 Run the project in a browser.

5 Click any of the restaurants in the horizontal list, and then click Reviews to see the updated data list with its new design-time data.

6 Close the browser and return to Flash Catalyst.

Add and delete design-time data

By default, the Data List component begins with five sample records. In some cases, this may not be enough to demonstrate the list effectively. For example, a list that will eventually display a large collection of thumbnail images may need a larger sample to activate the scroll bar or to fill out the total area in a tiled set of images.

1 In the Design-Time Data panel, click row number 3 in the far-left column to select it. Be sure to click the row number, not one of its image or text columns.

Clicking the row number selects the row without opening the Select Asset dialog box.

2 Click Add Row in the Design-Time Data panel.

An exact copy of the selected row is added below it and any rows after that are renumbered. You can swap the images and text, just like you've done for the other rows.

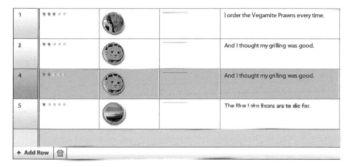

3 Select the new row you just added (it should be row 4), and click the Delete icon (🗑) in the Design-Time Data panel.

The row is deleted.

4 Collapse the Design-Time Data panel so you can see more of the artboard.

Add and remove elements in the repeated item

After creating the data list, you can modify the repeated item template by adding or removing text and images.

1 Select the Data List component and click Edit Parts in the HUD to edit the component in Edit-In-Place mode.

▶ **Tip:** To edit a Data List component in Edit-In-Place mode, you can double-click the data list. You can also select it and choose Modify > Edit Component. A third option is to select it and click Edit Parts in the HUD.

2 Double-click the repeated item (anywhere in the list of reviews).

3 In the Images category in the Library panel, locate the categoryIcon_Japanese.png file.

It's a little piece of sushi.

4 Drag the categoryIcon_Japanese.png file to the artboard and position it to the left of the stars.

Right now, the sushi graphic is only in the Normal state of the repeated item.

5 Choose States > Share To State > All States.

Now the sushi icon appears in the Normal, Over, and Selected states.

● **Note:** If you add new text in the repeated item, the option in the Design-Time Data section of the HUD changes to Add Text To Design-Time Data.

6 In the Design-Time Data section of the HUD, choose Add Image To Design-Time Data.

7 Click Review_Popup in the Breadcrumbs bar.

Every item in the data list now includes the sushi graphic.

8 Expand the Design-Time Data panel.

A new column, Image 4, is added to the Design-Time Data panel.

	Image 1	Image 2	Image 3	Image 4	Text 1
0	★★★★★				This is on
1	★★★★☆				Who doe
2	★★★☆☆				I order the
3	★★☆☆☆				And I tho
4	★☆☆☆☆				The Blue

+ Add Row

9 Click the Image 4 sushi graphic in row 1.

10 In the Select Asset dialog box, select categoryIcon_Cafe.png and click OK.

The sushi is now a cup of coffee.

11 Collapse the Design-Time Data panel.

The icons are updated in the list.

12 Double-click the Data List component to edit it in Edit-In-Place mode.

13 Double-click the repeated item (anywhere in the list of reviews) to edit it.

14 Select the sushi graphic

15 In the HUD, choose Remove Image From Design-Time Data.

The image is no longer part of the design-time data, but it still appears in the artboard.

16 Select the sushi graphic, open the Layers panel, and click the Delete icon (🗑) in the Layers panel to remove it from the application.

17 Close the project without saving changes and leave Flash Catalyst open.

> ▶ **Tip:** You can also add or remove repeated item template images and text by choosing Modify > Add Image (or Text) To Design-Time Data; or choosing Modify > Remove From Design-Time Data.

Using a wireframe data list

For rapid design of a traditional-looking data list, you can use the built-in Data List component in the Wireframe Components panel.

1 Open a new blank Flash Catalyst document.

2 Open the Wireframe Components panel and drag the Data List component to the artboard.

A wireframe data list appears. It starts with a single column of text, and the Design-Time Data panel opens automatically.

You can use the Design-Time Data panel to change the text and add or remove rows.

3 Double-click the wireframe data list to edit it in Edit-In-Place mode.

The wireframe data list includes horizontal and vertical scroll bars. The scroll bars become visible if the list is too long or too wide to display the data in the area defined by the repeated item bounding box.

4 Double-click the list to edit the repeated item.

As with all data lists, the repeated item has Normal, Over, and Selected states. You can modify the repeated item as needed. For example, you can add new text and widen the bounding box to create additional columns in the data table.

5 Close the project without saving changes.

Review questions

1 What are the two types of elements that can be represented by design-time data?

2 What is the required part that every Data List component must have?

3 What are three layout options for a data list repeated item?

4 Where in the Flash Catalyst Design workspace do you add and replace design-time data?

5 What types of changes can you make to the repeated item template that are reflected in every list item or record at runtime?

6 After creating a data list, is it possible to add or remove images and text in the repeated item?

7 What is the fastest way to add a traditional-looking data list (one that resembles a table or worksheet) to your application?

Review answers

1 Bitmap images and text can be represented by design-time data. The Design-Time Data panel is used to indicate which bitmap images and text to display in each sample record of the data list.

2 Every Data List component must include a master item called the *repeated item*. The repeated item is a *template* that defines the appearance of every item or record in the list, including its Normal, Over, and Selected states.

3 Horizontal, Vertical, and Tile are the layout options for a data list.

4 Using the Design-Time Data panel, you can replace the sample repeated images and text with more realistic examples of the actual data that you want displayed. This dummy data is called design-time data.

5 You can change the layout of the repeated item. You can change the appearance of the Normal, Over, and Selected states in the repeated item. You can edit properties for each object in the repeated item.

6 Yes. After creating the data list, you can modify the repeated item template by adding or removing text and images. This is done by editing the repeated item in Edit-In-Place mode, selecting the item you want to add or remove, and then using the HUD or the Modify menu to add or remove the item as design-time data.

7 For rapid design of a traditional-looking data list, use the built-in Data List component in the Wireframe Components panel.

11 DRAWING AND EDITING ARTWORK

Lesson Overview

When it comes to designing application prototypes, or for creating simple icons, background shapes, panels, and buttons, you'll find everything you need right here in Flash Catalyst.

If you have a copy of Adobe Photoshop CS5 or Adobe Illustrator CS5 installed, you can also take advantage of the Flash Catalyst integrated round-trip editing features. Select the artwork you want to edit, launch Illustrator or Photoshop, and then return the edited artwork to Flash Catalyst. The artwork maintains its exact location in the application.

In this lesson, you'll learn how to do the following:

- Use the rulers, guides, and grid

- Draw basic shapes and lines

- Change stroke and fill settings

- Add and modify gradient fills

- Group and position objects

- Apply and remove filters

- Launch and edit using Photoshop CS5 and Illustrator CS5

 This lesson will take about 90 minutes to complete. Copy the Lesson11 folder into the lessons folder that you created on your hard drive for these projects (or create it now), if you haven't already done so. As you work on this lesson, you won't be preserving the start files; if you need to restore the start files, copy them from the *Adobe Flash Catalyst CS5 Classroom in a Book* CD.

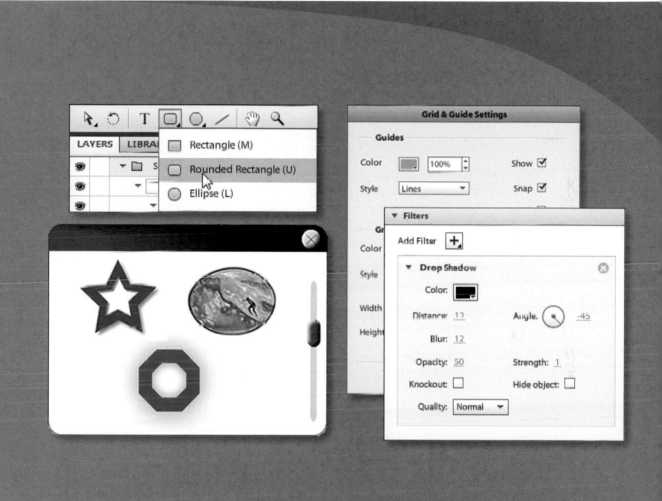

Flash Catalyst includes a set of tools for creating and modifying basic shapes and text. These tools are typically used for rapid prototyping of applications. Other uses include customizing the built-in wireframe components or quickly adding elements that don't require the advanced features of a Creative Suite application.

Flash Catalyst drawing tools

The shapes you create with the drawing tools are vector graphics. Text in Flash Catalyst is also a vector, but you'll be focusing on shapes in this exercise.

Some tools share the same location in the Tools panel. To select a hidden tool, click and hold down the mouse button to open the pop-up menu and then select a tool.

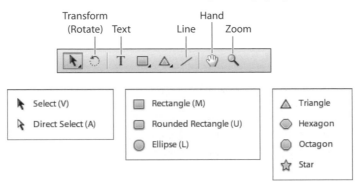

Select (dark arrow): Select, move, and size grouped or ungrouped objects.

Direct Select (light arrow): Select, move, and size objects that are part of a group.

Transform (Rotation): Size and rotate grouped and ungrouped objects.

Text: Dragging creates text that is confined within the box you drew, while clicking to place an insertion point creates text that can grow indefinitely in width as you type.

Rectangle: Drag to draw rectangles. Hold down Shift to draw a perfect square.

Rounded Rectangle: Drag to draw a rectangle with rounded corners. Hold down Shift to draw squares with rounded corners.

Ellipse: Drag to draw an ellipse. Hold down Shift to draw a perfect circle.

Triangle: Drag to draw a triangle. Move the mouse to the right or left to rotate the shape as you draw. Hold down Shift to rotate the triangle at 45-degree increments as you draw.

Hexagon: Drag to draw a hexagon. Move the mouse to the right or left to rotate the shape as you draw.

Octagon: Drag to draw an octagon. Move the mouse to the right or left to rotate the shape as you draw.

Star: Drag to draw a five-point star. Move the mouse to the right or left to rotate the shape as you draw.

Line: Drag to draw a straight line. Move the mouse to the right or left to rotate the line as you draw. Hold down Shift to rotate the line at 45-degree increments as you draw.

Hand: Drag to pan the artboard. This is a fast way of scrolling left and right in the artboard.

Zoom: Click in the artboard to zoom in for a closer view. Alt/Option-click to zoom back out. The zoom tool is synchronized with the Zoom Magnification box above the artboard.

Using the rulers, guides, and grid

Flash Catalyst offers four main aids to assist you while drawing. These include the rulers, the custom guides, a visible grid for measuring and aligning artwork, and the Properties panel for positioning and sizing objects down to the exact pixel.

Show and hide rulers

By default, rulers appear above and to the left of the artboard. The rulers help you position artwork, but they're even more useful when placing custom guides. You can hide the rulers to gain a little extra room in the workspace, but they take up so little space you'll probably want to leave them turned on all the time.

1 Browse to the Lesson11 folder on your hard drive and open the Lesson11_Drawing.fxp file.

   Rulers appear above and to the left of the artboard in the Design workspace.

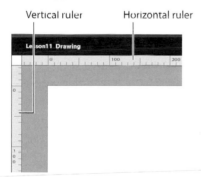

2 Choose View > Show Rulers to deselect it and hide the rulers.

   The rulers disappear, creating a little more space above and to the left of the artboard.

3   Choose View > Show Rulers to turn the rulers back on.

Rulers measure the height and width of the artboard in pixels. At 100% magnification, tick marks appear every 10 pixels and numbers appear at 100-pixel intervals.

4   Change the Zoom Magnification to 800%.

As you zoom in or out, the tick marks and numbers in the ruler scale to accommodate the new magnification.

5   Return the zoom magnification to 100%.

Edit grid and guide settings

Using the grid is similar to placing a transparent sheet of graph paper over the artboard. The grid includes perfectly spaced vertical and horizontal lines that help you align and draw perfectly measured artwork. You can change the default settings for all grid lines and guides in one location—the Grid & Guide Settings dialog box.

1   Open the View menu and point to Grid.

The Grid submenu appears. You can show and hide the grid or turn the Snap To Grid feature on and off. Selecting Snap To Grid causes objects to snap tightly up against the nearest gridline when you position them in the artboard.

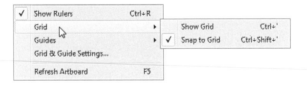

2   In the View menu, point to Guides.

The Guides submenu appears. You can show and hide the guides, lock the guides in place, turn the Snap To Guides feature on and off, or clear all guides from the application.

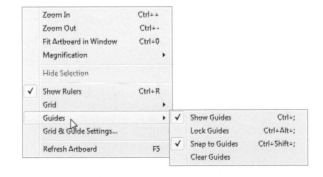

3 In the View menu, choose Grid & Guide Settings.

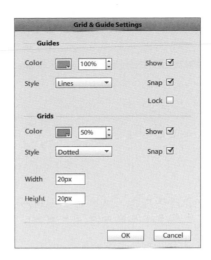

The Grid & Guide Settings dialog box appears. You can change the color, opacity, and style (straight dotted lines) for the grid and guides. You can adjust the scale of the grid by changing the Width and Height values. The default is a 20 x 20 pixel grid. You can show or hide the grid and guides or turn snapping on and off. You can also lock and unlock the guide lines.

4 In the Guides section, select Show and Snap. Make sure that Lock is deselected.

5 In the Grid section of the dialog box, change the opacity to 50%.

Reducing the opacity to 50% makes the grid lines less distracting as you draw new shapes and lines.

6 In the Grid section, select Show and Snap.

7 Make sure the grid Height and Width are both set to 20px.

8 Click OK to confirm the settings and close the dialog box.

The grid appears at 50% opacity in the artboard.

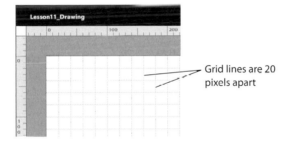

Grid lines are 20 pixels apart

Set guides for precise drawing

Guides are another great tool for aligning and placing one or more objects in the artboard. Unlike the grid, you can place horizontal or vertical guides anywhere you want. Use the ruler for exact placement of your custom guides. The same guides persist across all pages in the application.

1 Move the pointer over the top (horizontal) ruler.

2 Drag toward the artboard. You will see a horizontal guide appear. Release the mouse button to place the guide in the artboard.

▶ **Tip:** The guides you set for the main pages in the application do not appear when you edit a component in Edit-In-Place mode. When a component is in Edit-In-Place mode, you can place new guides that are unique to that component.

3 Select the Select tool (dark arrow) in the Tools panel.

4 Position the pointer over the guide. The pointer changes to a two-headed arrow. Drag the guide so that it's positioned at exactly 100 pixels from the top of the artboard, as shown in the vertical ruler.

▶ **Tip:** To remove a single guide, drag it off the artboard.

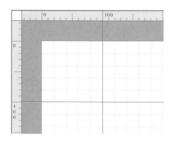

5 Move the pointer over the left (vertical) ruler.

6 Drag a vertical guide into the artboard and place it at 100 pixels from the left edge, as shown in the top (horizontal) ruler.

7 Add two more guides: a vertical guide at 500 pixels and a horizontal guide at 400 pixels.

Using guides, you've created boundaries for a 400 x 300 panel that you're going to draw using basic shapes and lines.

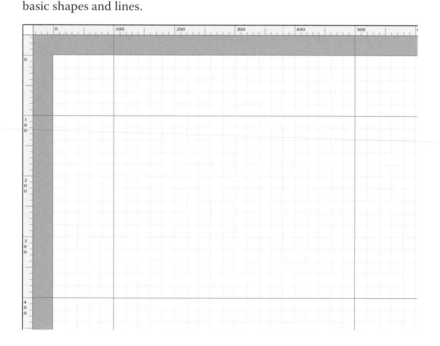

▶ **Tip:** To clear all guides from the application, choose View > Guides > Clear Guides. Guides that you've set inside a component are not affected. To remove guides in a component, edit the component in Edit-In-Place mode and then clear the guides.

8 Choose View > Guides > Lock Guides.

Locking the guides prevents them from being accidentally moved when selecting and positioning objects in the artboard.

Drawing basic shapes and lines

For most designers, using the Flash Catalyst drawing tools is a cinch. For anyone new to vector drawing tools, you'll find the best way to master them is to practice. A little experimentation, combined with the Undo command, goes a long way.

Preview a drawing example

In this exercise, you are going to draw a simple user interface panel. Before you get started, take a look at a sample of the finished panel.

1 Make sure Panel is selected in the Pages/States panel.

2 In the Layers panel, show the Sample Panel row.

Here is an example of a simple control panel that was created using basic shapes and lines. You are going to create a similar panel using the Flash Catalyst drawing tools.

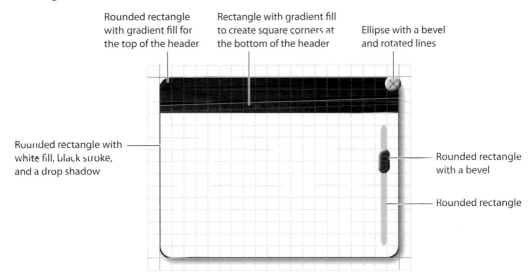

Rounded rectangle with gradient fill for the top of the header

Rectangle with gradient fill to create square corners at the bottom of the header

Ellipse with a bevel and rotated lines

Rounded rectangle with white fill, black stroke, and a drop shadow

Rounded rectangle with a bevel

Rounded rectangle

3 Hide the Sample Panel row in the Layers panel.

Draw rectangles

You can draw rectangles with square or rounded corners. There are two ways to create a rounded rectangle. You can use the Rounded Rectangle tool, or you can draw a standard rectangle using the Rectangle tool and then adjust the Corners value in the Properties panel.

1 In the Tools panel, select the Rectangle tool.

2 Position the pointer at the upper-left corner of the intersecting guides. Drag to the lower-right corner of the intersecting guides to draw a 400 x 300 rectangle.

As you draw, the edges of the shape snap to the guides.

In the Common section of the Properties panel, you see the properties for the rectangle. The width (W) is 400 and the height (H) is 300. If it's not, then adjust it in the Properties panel.

The guides make it easy to draw, but difficult to see the result in the artboard.

3 Choose View > Guides > Show Guides to hide the guides.

4 In the Properties panel, change the Corners value to **20**.

The Panel Background now has rounded corners.

5 In the Layers panel, rename the Rectangle **Panel Background**.

▶ **Tip:** When drawing shapes, you can use the grid to size the shape. For example, if grid lines are 20 pixels high and Snap To Grid is turned on, a rectangle that is three rows high has a height of 60 pixels.

6 Above the first rectangle, draw another one that's 400 pixels wide and 60 pixels tall. Change the Corners value to **20**. Then, in the Layers panel, name the second rectangle **Panel Header**.

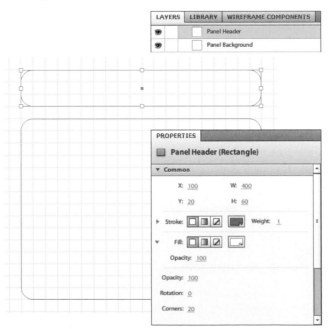

7 Below the Panel Background, draw another rectangle that's exactly 400 pixels wide by 30 pixels high. You can adjust its final size in the Properties panel if needed. Leave the Corners value set to 0.

8 In the Layers panel, name the new rectangle **Header Overlay**. We'll use this to hide the rounded corners at the bottom of the header.

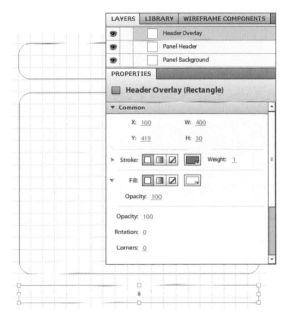

Now let's draw a track for the panel scroll bar.

Draw rounded rectangles

OK, so technically you've already drawn some rounded rectangles using the Rectangle tool and the Properties panel. But the Rounded Rectangle tool provides a shortcut by adding rounded corners automatically.

1 Select the Rounded Rectangle tool.

2 Draw a tall rectangle that's 200 pixels high and about 10 pixels wide (halfway between two grid lines). In the Layers panel, name the rectangle **Track.**

By default, the corner radius is 10, which is fine for the scroll bar track.

▶ **Tip:** To move a shape or grouped objects, use the Select tool. To select and move a single object within a group, use the Direct Select tool.

▶ **Tip:** You can change between shape tools by using their shortcut keys. For example, to select the Rectangle tool, press M. To select the Rounded Rectangle, press U. To select the Ellipse tool, press L.

3 Using the Select tool (dark arrow) in the Tools panel, drag the Track rectangle to position it along the inside lower-right edge of the larger rectangle.

Next, we'll draw a thumb for the scroll bar.

4 Using the Rounded Rectangle tool, draw a small rounded rectangle that overlaps the track. Make it about 20 pixels wide by 40 pixels high.

5 In the Layers panel, name the small rectangle **Thumb**.

You now have five rectangles that make up the shapes you need to build the panel. You're going to add some style and position these elements in a moment, but first you'll create some shapes for the panel close button.

Draw ellipses

To create a close button for the panel, let's start by drawing a large circle. We'll make it big at first and then scale it down later. To draw a perfect circle, use the Ellipse tool with the Shift key modifier.

1 Select the Ellipse tool in the Tools panel.

2 Hold down Shift and drag to draw a perfect circle that's 200 x 200 pixels. In the grid, that's a circle that is 10 rows high and 10 rows wide. You might find that it's easier to draw the circle and then change its size in the Properties panel.

The ellipse is a perfect circle.

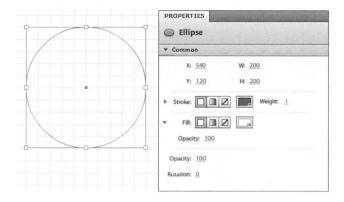

Draw basic lines

The close button should have an X in the middle. Let's use the grid to draw a perfect plus sign, and then we'll rotate the entire button to turn the plus sign into an X.

1 Select the Line tool in the Tools panel.

2 Position the pointer 20 pixels (one grid line) below the top of the circle, in the center. Drag to draw a vertical line that's 160 pixels high. You can hold down Shift as you draw to make a perfectly vertical line.

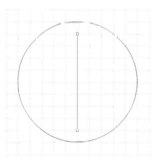

3 Position the pointer 10 pixels inside the left edge of the circle, in the center. Drag to draw a horizontal line that's about 160 pixels wide. You can hold down Shift as you draw to make a perfectly horizontal line.

You now have the basic shapes for the panel close button. You'll rotate this in a moment.

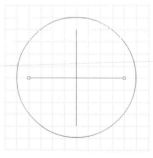

Changing stroke and fill

If drawing basic shapes is like making a coloring book, then changing fill and stroke is the fun part. You get to color in the pictures. Flash Catalyst lets you choose between no fill (transparent), solid fill, and gradients that fade between one or more colors at various angles. Even the stroke (outline) can be a gradient if it has enough weight. Weight refers to the width or thickness of the stroke. All of these changes are made in the Common section of the Properties panel.

Change the fill color

When you first start Flash Catalyst, new shapes are created with a solid white fill. But as soon as you change the fill color of a shape, any new shape that you draw takes on the most recent fill color that you've applied.

1   Using the Select tool (dark arrow), click the Panel Background rectangle (the largest rectangle) to select it.

The properties for the selected shape appear in the Properties panel. The fill color is solid white.

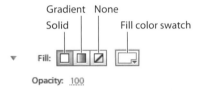

2   Select the Panel Header rectangle.

3   In the Properties panel, click the Fill color swatch to open the Color Picker.

In the Color Picker, you can select a color in the palette or enter a hexadecimal color value. For additional colors, drag the slider (right-pointing arrow) up or down to select a new color range and then drag in the color field to select a new color. You can also sample a color in the application by using the Eyedropper tool.

4   In the color palette, select blue #2B4381.

5   Select the Header Overlay and Thumb rectangles.

▶ **Tip:** Shift-click to select multiple objects in the artboard, or contiguous rows in the Layers panel. But Ctrl/Command-click to select noncontiguous rows in the Layers panel.

With Header Overlay and Thumb selected, you can apply the same properties to both shapes at the same time.

6 In the Properties panel, click the Fill color swatch to open the Color Picker, and select the Eyedropper tool.

7 With the Eyedropper tool selected, move the pointer over the blue Panel Header rectangle and click to sample its color.

The Color Picker disappears and the blue color you sampled is applied to the Header Overlay and Thumb shapes.

8 Select the Track rectangle and the Ellipse.

9 In the Properties panel, click the Fill color swatch and select light gray #CCCCCC.

The scroll bar track and the Ellipse are light gray.

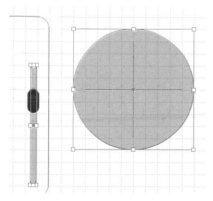

Understanding hexadecimal color values

The colors you see on your computer monitor are produced using various combinations of red, green, and blue (RGB). You may have noticed the numbers in the Color Picker. These are referred to as hexadecimal color codes. Hexadecimal color codes define the amounts of red, green, and blue used to create a color. The levels of red, green, and blue are measured using a numbering system that runs from 0 to 255. For example, the color black is created by mixing 0 red, 0 green, and 0 blue. White is represented by 255 red, 255 green, and 255 blue. Yellow is 255 each of red and green, and 0 blue.

While RGB color values are based on the decimal system (base 10), hexadecimal color values are represented by a hexadecimal numbering system (base 16).

In the decimal system, when you write 43 it means 4 tens and 3 ones. When you write 43 in hexadecimal it means 4 sixteens and 3 ones. 43 in hexadecimal is (4x16) + 3 = 67.

In hexadecimal, A = 10, B = 11, C = 12, and so on to F, which is 15. The highest possible two-digit number in hexadecimal is FF. It means 15 sixteens and 15 ones, which is 255 (the most amount of any color).

Hexadecimal color codes always consist of a number sign (#) followed by a combination of six characters.

- The first two digits determine how much red is in the color.
- The middle two digits determine how much green is in the color.
- The last two digits determine how much blue is in the color.
- The code for black is #000000.

Colors containing RGB values of FF contain the most amount of a color (255 or 100%). For example, the hexadecimal value for white is #FFFFFF, which means it contains the most amount of red, green and blue.

When specifying colors in a web application, you can use hexadecimal values instead of RGB values. An advantage of using hexadecimal codes to choose colors is that you can limit your design's color palette to colors that are considered safe for viewing on the web. Web-safe colors consist of any three of the pairs 00, 33, 66, 99, CC, or FF in the hexadecimal range. For example, #FF9900 is a web-safe color, whereas #39C6C5 does not appear in the web-safe color palette.

The importance of these safe colors has been reduced dramatically over the years as display monitors have become more capable of displaying many colors.

Change stroke color and weight

Stroke is the line or outline that defines a shape you draw in Flash Catalyst—as in the "stroke of the pen" or "brush strokes." In Flash Catalyst, you can choose a solid stroke, a gradient stroke, or no stroke at all.

A gradient is when two or more colors gradually blend together. A gradient stroke may seem strange, but if you make the weight of the stroke heavy enough, it becomes almost like an outer shape surrounding an inner shape.

Solid stroke   Gradient stroke   No stroke

Our panel design doesn't require any fancy gradient strokes, but we do need to make a few minor modifications, beginning with the panel background.

1   Select the Panel Background rectangle (the larger rectangle).

2   In the Properties panel, make sure the Solid Stroke property is selected. Click the Stroke color swatch, and change the stroke color to black **#000000**.

3   Change the Weight value to 2.

4   Use the Layers panel to select the Ellipse, Thumb, Track, Header Overlay, and Panel Header.

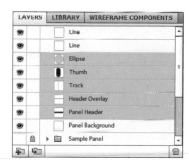

5   In the Properties panel, click the No Stroke property to remove the stroke from all five selected shapes.

Note: Removing the stroke from a rectangle reduces its overall height and width.

6 Choose Edit > Deselect All so that you can see the change a little better.

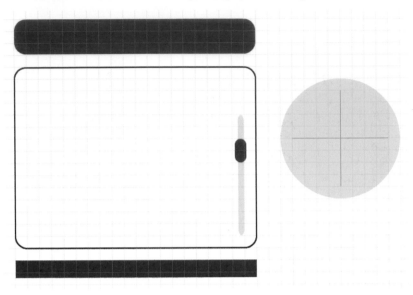

Add and modify gradient fills

Let's add a gradient fill to the Panel Header and the Header Overlay. Then, we'll place the overlay on top of the header to hide the bottom rounded corners.

1 Select the Panel Header rectangle.

2 In the Properties panel, select the Gradient fill property.

A gradient swatch displays a preview of the gradient from left to right. Beneath the swatch are gradient color stops. They're called stops because they control where one color stops and the next one begins.

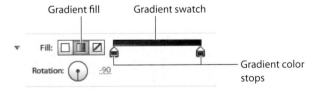

By default, there are two color stops. The first stop is the current shape's fill color (blue). The last stop is black. The artboard shows a gradient fade from blue to black.

3 Click anywhere in the gradient swatch to add another color stop.

A new color stop takes on the color of the stop to its left.

4 Click directly on the new stop to open the Color Picker.

You can change the color and the opacity of each color stop.

5 Select white in the color palette.

The new stop color is white. In the artboard, the fill color fades from blue to white and then to black.

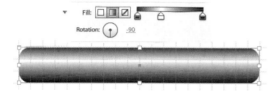

6 Drag the white color stop left and right to see how this affects the gradient fill in the artboard.

You can add more color stops. You can also move the first and last stops to adjust where the fades begin and end.

7 Drag the white color stop (and any other extra stops you've added) away from the gradient swatch to remove it.

You're back to where you started, with a blue and black color stop.

● **Note:** You cannot remove stops when there are only two stops left. You can remove the first or last stops as long as other stops exist in the middle.

8 In the Properties panel, change the Fill Rotation value to **80**. Make sure you change the Fill Rotation, not the Rotation for the shape.

The gradient fades from blue to black at an angle, making it a little more interesting.

9 Select the Header Overlay rectangle.

10 In the Properties panel, select the Gradient Fill property and change its Fill Rotation value to **80**.

The same blue to black gradient is added to the Header Overlay rectangle.

11 Shift-click the Panel Header rectangle to add it to the selection.

12 With both parts of the header selected, choose Modify > Align > Bottom. Then choose Modify > Align > Left.

13 Choose Edit > Deselect All.

14 Choose View > Grid > Show Grid to deselect it and hide the grid.

The combined shapes make a panel header that's square on the bottom with rounded top corners. The shapes are different sizes so the gradient rotation creates a seam. To hide the seam, you can change the Rotation value for one of the shapes until the gradient patterns line up perfectly.

Note: If you select multiple objects with different gradients (or some with no gradients), the properties show that no gradient is applied. Clicking the blank gradient swatch resets all items to the default black-and-white gradient.

15 Select the Header Overlay rectangle (the smaller of the two rectangles). In the Properties panel, change the Fill Rotation value to **5**.

16 Choose Edit > Deselect All.

The gradient patterns line up and the seam is gone.

Note: A checkerboard pattern in the gradient swatch indicates areas of transparency.

Grouping and transforming

Most artwork is made from a collection of smaller overlapping parts. In fact, some artwork includes hundreds, even thousands, of smaller brush strokes or paths. You can make your life a little easier by grouping the related parts of an object so that you can work with them as a single unit.

The following are a few benefits of grouping objects:

- Grouping protects the integrity of the drawing by keeping its parts in their correct position relative to its other parts.

- Grouping creates a nicely organized Group object in the Layers panel. You can rename the group in the Layers panel for better organization.

- Grouped objects have their own set of properties in the Properties panel, which makes it easier to size, position, and transform the drawing. For example, you can change its opacity, rotate the drawing, or apply filters.

- You can use the Select tool to select, transform, size, and position the group as a single unit.

- You can always select the parts within a group by using the Direct Select tool, or by selecting their individual rows in the Layers panel.

Tip: If your drawings include lots of smaller parts or paths, you can group them, select the group, and use the Heads-Up Display (HUD) to create an optimized graphic.

Group objects

The panel you're creating includes the rounded Panel Header and Header Overlay rectangles. You've already aligned these objects perfectly, so let's go ahead and group them. That'll make it easier to position them at the top of the panel. While we're at it, let's also group the ellipse and lines used to make the close button. This will make rotating, sizing, and positioning these parts a lot easier too.

1   Select the Panel Header and Header Overlay rectangles.

2   Choose Modify > Group.

   The two gradient rectangles are grouped and share one set of selection handles.

3   In the Layers panel, rename the group **Panel Header**.

4   Select the Ellipse shape and the two lines.

5   Choose Modify > Group.

6   In the Layers panel, rename the group **Close**.

Transform shapes

Let's use the Transform tool to rotate the close button and turn the plus sign into an X for "close."

1   In the Layers panel, select the Close group.

2   Select the Transform (Rotate) tool in the Tools panel.

   Transform handles appear around the group.

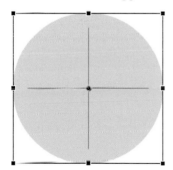

3   Position the pointer over the selected shapes.

   The pointer changes to the Transform tool.

4   Drag to rotate the selected shapes by 45 degrees.

   The Rotation value changes in the Properties panel.

5   In the Properties panel, make sure the Rotation value is exactly 45 or -45 to turn the crossed lines into an X.

Note: You can also use the transform tool to resize or rotate other objects, such as a bitmap image or vector drawing that you've imported.

Size and position objects

With our shapes grouped, we can move and size them as single drawings. Let's start by putting the header at the top of the panel, just inside the outline of the panel background. After that, we'll reduce the size of the close button and place it where it belongs, at the top of the panel.

1   Using the Select tool (dark arrow), drag the grouped Panel Header to position it at the top inside the Panel Background rectangle.

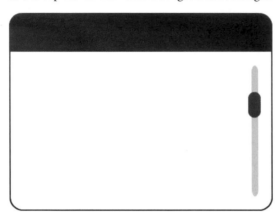

2   Select the Close group in the Layers panel.

3   Hold down the Shift key, then drag a corner selection handle to reduce the size of the Close group. Make it small enough to fit in the upper-right corner of the panel header. It doesn't need to be exact.

▶ **Tip:** You can press the arrow keys to move an object 1 pixel at a time. Holding down Shift when you press the arrow keys moves the object 10 pixels at a time.

4   Position the Close group in the upper-right corner of the panel.

Applying and removing filters

Flash Catalyst includes a nice collection of graphic filters, such as drop shadows, that you can add to your artwork to give it more depth and style. You can add filters to the artwork you place in the Flash Catalyst artboard. For example, you can apply filters to the vector drawings and bitmap images you import to the project, as well as to the vector shapes you create using the Flash Catalyst drawing tools. You can even add filters to text.

You can apply the following filters in the Properties panel: Blur, Drop Shadow, Inner Shadow, Bevel, Glow, and Inner Glow.

After you apply a filter, additional filter settings appear in the Properties panel.

● **Note:** If an object has different filters applied in two states, you cannot animate the change between filters during transitions. The change occurs immediately during the transition.

Add and modify a bevel

A bevel filter creates a raised, or beveled, edge, giving the object the appearance of depth. By adding bevel filters to the close button and the scroll bar thumb, we can create the illusion of three-dimensional objects.

1   Zoom the artboard to 200% and pan the artboard so that you can see both the Close group and the scroll bar Thumb shape.

2   Select the Close group.

3   In the Filters section of the Properties panel, click Add Filter and choose Bevel.

    A bevel is applied to the selection. The filter properties appear in the Properties panel.

4   Change the Distance value to **4**.

5   Change the Blur value to **6**.

6   Change the Angle value to **−45**.

7   Change the Strength value to **1**.

8   Select the Thumb shape. Apply a bevel with the same properties as the Close group.

▶ **Tip:** You can set the quality of a filter in the Properties panel. The options include Low, Normal, and High. Increasing quality increases the file size of the application. The Normal quality is usually a good choice.

9   Change the artboard back to 100% magnification.

Add and modify a drop shadow

The most common type of filter is the drop shadow. Using drop shadows adds style and depth and gives a softer look to artwork and text. By adjusting the direction and distance of the shadow, you create the perception of lighting.

Adding a shadow to the Panel Background rectangle will give it the appearance that it's floating slightly above the main user interface.

1   Select the Panel Background rectangle.

2   In the Filter section of the Properties panel, click Add Filter and choose Drop Shadow.

A drop shadow is applied to the selection. The filter properties appear in the Properties panel.

3   Change the Distance value to **10**.

4   Change the Blur value to **10**.

5   Change the Opacity value to **60**.

6   Change the Angle value to **–45**.

7   Change the Strength value to **1**.

8   Choose Edit > Deselect All.

The panel is complete.

▶ **Tip:** The Knockout Drop Shadow property hides the original object, but it shows only the parts of the filter that would be seen if the object were visible (the filter is masked/knocked out by the object). Hide Object hides the original object and shows the filter, including parts that would have been obscured if the object were visible. This has no effect if Knockout is also selected.

Round-trip editing with Adobe Illustrator and Adobe Photoshop

Using the Launch and Edit features of Flash Catalyst, you can modify artwork using the rich editing capabilities of Adobe Illustrator CS5 and Adobe Photoshop CS5. Open the artwork in Illustrator or Photoshop, make changes, and then return to Flash Catalyst.

Take a moment to review the following tips for round-trip editing with Illustrator and Photoshop:

- Use Illustrator to round-trip edit bitmaps and vectors.

- Use Photoshop to round-trip edit bitmaps.

- When you edit a vector (shape or text) in Illustrator and the vector is not part of a component, changes apply only to the state in which you select and edit the vector. If the vector was shared to other states, they are not affected by the edit

- When you edit an image or component that is stored in the Flash Catalyst library, you are editing the object definition in the library. If you've shared the image across states, the changes apply in all states. If the image is used inside a component, the changes are reflected in the component.

- You cannot round-trip edit vectors or bitmaps that you've optimized by choosing Optimize Vector Graphics in the HUD.

- You cannot round-trip edit more than one component at a time.

- Make all structural changes to objects in Flash Catalyst. Changing the structure of objects during round-trip editing can break the intended behavior of objects or transitions in which they occur.

- When you round-trip edit a button (or other components), the component states are shown as separate layers in Illustrator and Photoshop. If you round-trip edit a group, its children are shown as separate layers.

- When you round-trip edit an object, the surrounding objects in the artboard are visible (but dimmed) for reference. These objects appear as locked background layers in Illustrator and Photoshop and cannot be edited.

Launch and edit in Adobe Illustrator

Using Illustrator, you can edit drawings, as well as the following components: Button, Checkbox, Radio Button, Horizontal Scrollbar, Vertical Scrollbar, Text Input, Toggle Button, Horizontal Slider, or Vertical Slider. You cannot round-trip edit Custom/Generic components.

To complete this exercise, you must have Adobe Illustrator CS5 installed.

1   Select LaunchAI in the Pages/States panel.

This page includes a sample drawing of a wrench that was created using basic shapes. This would look better if the wrench handle tapered inward a little near the head of the wrench. To do this, you need to edit the anchor points of the handle shape, which cannot be done in Flash Catalyst. To make this change, you can launch Adobe Illustrator CS5 and edit the path using the Adobe Illustrator Pen tool. The shapes that make up the wrench are grouped.

2   Use the Direct Select tool (light arrow) to select the wrench handle.

3   Choose Modify > Edit in Adobe Illustrator CS5.

Adobe Illustrator CS5 starts, and the shape you selected appears in the Illustrator artboard. This is similar to Edit-In-Place mode in Flash Catalyst. Only the selected artwork can be edited. The other artwork appears in the background for reference only.

A message at the top of the Illustrator window tells you that you are editing from Adobe Flash Catalyst.

4   Use the Illustrator Direct Select tool to select the shape.

5 Click the anchor point at the upper-left side of the shape.

Handles appear. You can modify points on a path in Illustrator.

6 Drag the upper-left anchor point to the right slightly to taper the top portion of the wrench handle.

7 Drag the upper-right anchor point to the left slightly.

The wrench handle now gets narrower near the top of the wrench.

8 Click Done at the top of the application window.

The FXG Options dialog box appears.

9 Click OK to close the FXG Options dialog box and return to Flash Catalyst.

The changes you made in Illustrator appear in Flash Catalyst.

● **Note:** After launching artwork in Illustrator, you can click Cancel to close the application without making changes.

Download and install the Adobe FXG extensions for Photoshop

Before you can take advantage of round-trip editing with Adobe Photoshop, you need to download and install the FXG extensions. These include the FXG plug-in and the Simplify Layers For FXG script.

Instructions for downloading and installing the extensions are located at www. adobe.com/go/photoshopfxg.

Launch and edit in Adobe Photoshop

Use Photoshop to edit bitmap images, a selection of multiple images, or a group containing only images.

To complete this exercise, you must have Adobe Photoshop CS5 installed.

1 Select LaunchPS in the Pages/States panel.

2 Select the bitmap image of the surfer.

3 Choose > Modify > Edit In Adobe Photoshop CS5.

A message reminds you that you need to download and install the FXG extensions for Photoshop.

4 Click OK to close the message and launch Photoshop.

Adobe Photoshop CS5 starts, and the bitmap image you selected appears in the Photoshop canvas for editing. A message at the top of the canvas reminds you to run the script to simplify layers before returning to Flash Catalyst.

The image appears in its own layer in the Layers panel.

5 Select the layer for the image you're editing in the Photoshop Layers panel.

6 Choose Filter > Artistic > Dry Brush (or another filter of your choice).

7 Make any adjustments you want to the filter properties and click OK.

▶ **Tip:** When you're finished editing in Photoshop, save the image as a PSD file before running the Simplify Layers For FXG script. The PSD is your master file, preserving any layer effects (styles), adjustment layers, layer masks, smart objects, and so on, that you may have added.

8 Choose File > Scripts > Simplify Layers For FXG.

9 Choose File > Close and click Yes to save changes.

10 Return to Flash Catalyst.

The changes you made in Photoshop appear in the Flash Catalyst project.

Understanding blend modes

As you've been working in Flash Catalyst, you've probably noticed a property that's common to just about everything you select in the artboard, including components, bitmap images, imported vector drawings, text, and the shapes you draw. This is the Blend Modes property in the Appearance section of the Properties panel.

Blend modes are used to determine how layered objects blend together. It's helpful to think in terms of the following colors when visualizing a blend mode effect:

- The *base color* is the original color in the image.

- The *blend color* is the color being applied in a layer above it.

- The *result color* is the color resulting from the blend.

For more information on blend modes in Flash Catalyst, refer to the blend_modes. pdf document in the Lesson11 folder.

Review questions

1 What is the difference between the Select tool (dark arrow) and the Direct Select tool (light arrow)?

2 What are two methods for drawing rectangles with rounded corners?

3 When filling a shape with a solid color, how can you ensure that its color is an exact match to the color of another object in the artboard?

4 How do you control the colors used in a gradient fill?

5 What are some advantages of grouping objects?

6 When applying a Drop Shadow filter, what is the difference between the Knockout and Hide Object properties?

7 What are some differences between round-trip editing in Adobe Illustrator compared to round-trip editing in Adobe Photoshop?

Review answers

1 You can use the Select tool to select, move, and size grouped or ungrouped objects. You can use the Direct Select tool to select, move, and size objects that are part of a group.

2 You can draw a rectangle using the Rectangle tool and then add rounded corners by changing the Corners value in the Properties panel. You can draw a rectangle that begins with rounded corners by using the Rounded Rectangle tool.

3 You can use the Eyedropper tool to sample a color from another object in the artboard. Or, you can select the object that has the source color, open the Fill Color Picker, and copy the color's hexadecimal color value. Then, select the target object, open the Color Picker, and paste the color value. Using the Eyedropper is a lot easier.

4 Begin by adding a gradient fill in the Properties panel. The gradient begins with two colors—usually the fill color fading to black or white. Click a color stop below the gradient swatch to open the Color Picker and change its color. Click in the gradient swatch to add additional color stops. Slide color stops or adjust the Rotation value to stylize the gradient pattern. Drag stops away from the gradient swatch to remove them.

5 Grouping protects the integrity of the drawing by keeping its parts in their correct position relative to its other parts. Grouping creates a nicely organized Group object in the Layers panel. Grouped objects have their own set of properties. You can select, edit, size, and position the group as a single unit. You can add interactions to groups.

6 Knockout hides the original object, but it shows only the parts of the filter that would be seen if the object were visible (the filter is masked/knocked out by the object). Hide Object hides the original object and shows the filter, including parts that would have been obscured if the object were visible. This has no effect if Knockout is also selected.

7 You can use Illustrator to edit vectors and bitmaps. You can use Photoshop to edit bitmaps only. Before you can edit in Photoshop, you must download and install the FXG plug-in and the Simplify Layers For FXG script. After editing in Photoshop, make sure you run the Simplify Layers For FXG script before returning the edited graphic to Flash Catalyst.

12 PUBLISHING A PROJECT

Lesson Overview

You've created and imported artwork, designed interactive components, and built the application structure. Your project includes smooth animated transitions and sound effects. You've even added video that users can control, and now it's time to share your masterpiece with the world (or at least with your client—for review and feedback).

In this lesson, you'll learn how to do the following:

- Choose a delivery option

- Prepare the application for publishing

- Publish the application files

- View and share published files

- Publish to the web using Adobe Dreamweaver CS5

 This lesson will take about 40 minutes to complete. Copy the Lesson12 folder into the lessons folder that you created on your hard drive for these projects (or create it now), if you haven't already done so. As you work on this lesson, you won't be preserving the start files; if you need to restore the start files, copy them from the *Adobe Flash Catalyst CS5 Classroom in a Book* CD.

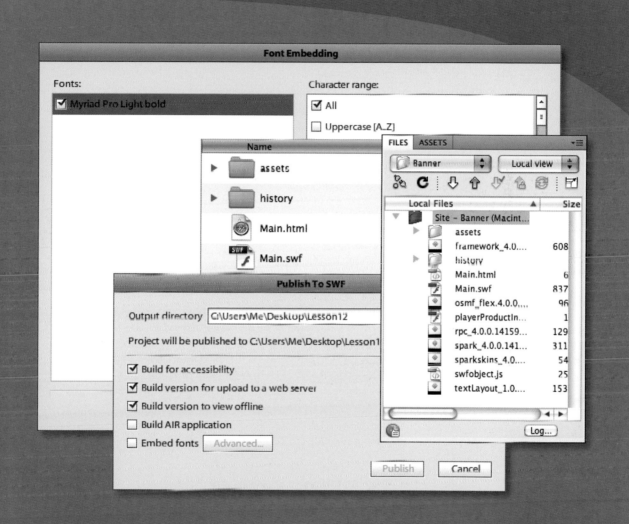

Export your finished project as a SWF file that leverages the ubiquity of Flash Player 10 or later. Output an offline version of the product for iterative design or client review. Publish to the web or create an Adobe AIR installation file and distribute the program as a desktop application.

Delivery options

There are three ways to publish and distribute a Flash Catalyst application. One version includes the necessary files to run the project as a web application, but cannot run locally. A second version can run locally, but cannot be run from a web server or launch URLs. There is also an option to build an Adobe AIR application. We'll refer to these as the *deploy-to-web*, *run-local*, and *AIR* versions of the application.

Deploy-to-web produces a smaller SWF file, along with the Flex 4 framework files. This version includes everything you need to publish the application to a web server for viewing online.

Run-local is a larger SWF file with all of its assets included and no dependencies. The purpose of this redistributable version is to share it. For example, you can share the file with a client and they'll have everything they need to view the application locally.

AIR is a stand-alone desktop application that runs without a web browser or Internet connection. Flash Catalyst publishes a single AIR application file used to download and install the application.

● **Note:** For applications that require additional work by a Flex developer, you'll save and share the Flash Catalyst project file (.fxp). The project file contains all the assets and code the developer needs to continue working with the project in Adobe Flash Builder.

Adobe AIR

With Adobe AIR, you can stop asking that nagging old question, "Will my application run the same on both Windows and Mac?" Yes. Adobe AIR is a cross-operating system runtime that allows you to build and deploy rich Internet applications (RIAs) to the desktop. Using Flash Catalyst, you can publish the project as an Adobe AIR application and then upload the published file to your web server. This allows someone to download and install the application locally. The application runs on the user's desktop without a web browser or an Internet connection.

The user installs the AIR runtime once on their computer. After that, they can install any number of AIR applications and use them just like any other desktop program.

The AIR runtime eliminates cross-browser testing by ensuring consistent functionality and interactions across desktops running Mac, Windows, or Linux.

● **Note:** Even with a data-centric project that requires further development in Flash Builder, you may want to publish preliminary versions of the application for sharing with clients or colleagues during the design and development workflow.

Publishing your application

When you publish a Flash Catalyst project, you choose which version(s) of the application to create. You can also choose to include accessibility features and whether or not to embed fonts.

Accessibility

Your Flash Catalyst projects are built for accessibility by default to support assistive technologies such as screen readers. This improves the user experience and makes projects readily apparent and easily navigable for visually impaired users. This capability is enabled through the Flex framework accessibility support. Including accessibility features in your project increases the size of the SWF file to accommodate the support. The only reason that you'd choose not to build for accessibility is to reduce the size of your published application.

Embedding fonts

You can make sure that everyone sees text as you've designed it to look by embedding fonts in the application's SWF file.

The main limitation to using embedded fonts is that embedded fonts increase the file size of your application.

Before you publish

It's always a good idea to do a little clean-up and test your projects before publishing. Take a look at the following pre-publishing ideas for optimizing your application.

- Delete objects that are not used in the application. If an object is not being used in a state, then select it and press the Delete key to remove it from the current state only. If an object is not used anywhere in the application, select it and click the Delete icon (🗑) in the Layers panel.

- Before publishing, you can optimize vector graphics by using the Optimize Artwork options in the Heads-Up Display (HUD) or by choosing Modify > Optimize Vector Graphics.

- To reduce the file size of the application, compress graphics in the Library panel. Right-click a graphic in the Library panel and choose Compression Options. Reduce the Quality setting and click OK.

- Your Flash Catalyst applications are Flex projects. Before publishing, you can switch over to the Code workspace and see how the components and states are created. You can also view the Problems panel in Code view to make sure that your project doesn't have any issues that need resolving.

- Run the project and test it before publishing. Check to make sure that all navigation and links are working properly. Preview all transitions to make sure they run smoothly. Test any video or sound controls.

- Save the project prior to publishing.

Publish to SWF

Let's publish the Interactive Banner application so that we can take a look at the publishing options and the different files that get produced.

1   Start Flash Catalyst, browse to the Lesson12 folder on your hard drive, and open the Lesson12_Banner.fxp file.

2   Choose File > Publish To SWF/AIR.

The options to Build For Accessibility, Build Version For Upload To A Web Server, and Build Version To View Offline are selected by default. You need to choose an Output Directory for the published files.

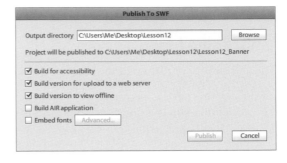

3   Click Browse and navigate to the Lesson12 folder on your hard drive. Select the Lesson12 folder and click OK/Open.

4   Select the Build AIR Application option.

5   Select the Embed Fonts option.

Selecting Embed Fonts activates the Advanced button.

6   Click Advanced to open the Font Embedding dialog box.

You can specify which fonts and character ranges to embed. For example, exclude specific language options, such as Greek and Thai. Limiting what you choose to embed can help reduce the size of your published SWF file.

● **Note:** If your project does not include fonts that you can embed, the Embed Fonts check box is disabled.

7 Click OK to accept the default font embedding settings.

8 Click Publish.

● **Note:** When you publish a project that has already been published, a message asks if you want to overwrite the existing files. You can choose Cancel and publish to a different directory, or choose Overwrite to replace the existing files.

When should I embed a font?

In general, don't embed fonts if you know that users already have them. To be safe, embed any fonts other than Arial, Courier New, Georgia, Times New Roman, and Verdana. Embedding non-web fonts ensures that users see the design exactly as you do, even if they don't have the same fonts on their computer. If you do embed fonts, use the Advanced button in the Publish To SWF dialog box to limit how much of the font is embedded. For example, if you know that your text includes only Basic Latin characters and numerals, then deselect the All option and select Uppercase, Lowercase, Numerals, Punctuation, and Basic Latin. Leave the remaining languages deselected.

Viewing the published files

Publishing a project generates the Main.swf file, along with any other files needed to run the application, depending on the options you select.

Flash Catalyst creates a new subfolder in the location you choose as the Output Directory. The new folder has the same name as your project file. Within that folder, you'll find a separate folder for each version of the application you choose to create—deploy-to-web, run-local, and AIR.

deploy-to-web is the folder containing the deployable web version of the application.

run-local is the folder containing the offline version of the application.

AIR is the folder containing the AIR application file.

1 Open the Lesson12 folder on your hard drive.

The folder includes the Output Directory with the same name as the project file, Lesson12_Banner.

2 Open the Lesson12_Banner Output Directory folder.

The three versions of your application are stored here.

▶ **Tip:** You can rename the deploy-to-web and other application folders to something more descriptive of your application. Keep in mind that if you rename the folder, republishing the project will not overwrite the previous version.

3 Open the deploy-to-web folder.

The deployable web version of the application includes all the necessary files to run the application from a web server. These are the files you upload to your web server if you want to deploy the application online.

● **Note:** Since Flash Player 9, the Flex framework files are cached by the Flash Player. Over time, most users will have the Flex framework as part of their Flash Player. In these cases, they'll just need to download the much smaller SWF file from your web server. But until then, it's best to put these files on your web server next to the SWF file.

The deploy-to-web files include the Main.swf application file and the main.html wrapper for the SWF file. This file references the swfobject.js code that performs Flash Player version checks and redirects a user to upgrade their Flash Player, if needed. If you choose to place the SWF file inside a different HTML page, you can copy and paste this code. The Flex framework files are also included and are external to the application SWF file. This helps to keep the size of the SWF file small, which is better for web delivery. The assets folder includes any linked assets. In the case of the Banner project, the sound and video files are stored here. All images are embedded in this project. The history folder includes a set of files that allow a Flex application to store browser history as you move from page to page within the application.

4 Close the deploy-to-web folder and open the run-local folder.

You can share the contents of the run-local folder with others to view the application. As long as they have Flash Player 10 or later installed, they can open the application in a web browser. In the run-local version of the application, the Flex framework is built into the SWF file. The reason for doing this is so that you can pass it around to someone else (a client) and they'll have everything they need to run the SWF file locally. The trade-off is that it makes the SWF file much bigger, but it has no external dependencies.

5 Double-click the Main.html file.

The Main.html file opens and loads the Main.swf file.

6 Close the browser.

7 Close the run-local folder and open the AIR folder.

The AIR folder includes one file. Anyone that has this file can install and run the AIR application.

8 Double-click the Lesson12_Banner.air file.

The Application Install dialog box opens. If the application was already installed, you'll have the option to run the installation again or uninstall the program.

● **Note:** Links to URLs don't work when viewing the run-local version of the application.

● **Note:** If you don't have the Adobe AIR runtime installed, or if your version of the AIR runtime needs updating, then you may need to install that first. Follow the prompts to install or update the AIR runtime if prompted.

9 Click Install.

The Installation options appear.

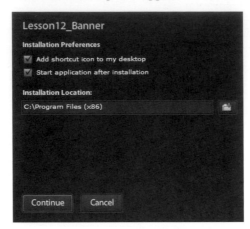

10 Make sure that Start Application After Installation is selected, and click Continue.

The program installs. When the installation is complete, the Lesson12_Banner application starts in a new application window.

11 Test the application by moving from page to page and viewing the videos on pages 4 and 5.

12 Close the application window.

13 Double-click the Lesson12_Banner.air file again.

The installer recognizes that you already have the application installed.

14 Click Uninstall.

The uninstaller removes the application from your computer.

15 When the application removal is complete, click Finish to close the dialog box.

Publishing to the web with Adobe Dreamweaver CS5

To deploy your published project to the web, upload the entire contents of the deploy-to-web folder to your web server. You can use a File Transfer Protocol (FTP) client, or use the site publishing and file management features within Adobe Dreamweaver CS5.

There are three main steps to publishing to the web using Dreamweaver:

1. Start Dreamweaver and create a new site. To do this, you create a local root folder and site structure.

2. Connect to the remote site.

3. Upload the Flash Catalyst application files.

Create a local root folder and site structure

A local root folder is a folder on your computer that holds subfolders and files for the website. It's like a staging area.

When you publish a Flash Catalyst application, the deploy-to-web folder is the local root folder on your hard drive.

1 Start Adobe Dreamweaver CS5.

2 Choose Site > New Site.

The Site Setup dialog box opens.

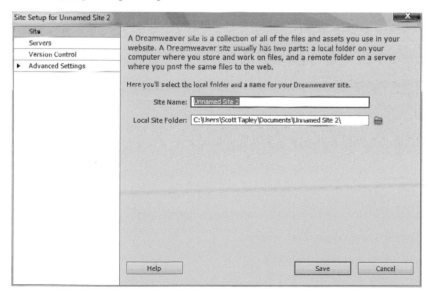

▶ **Tip.** When you start Dreamweaver, you can also choose Dreamweaver Site in the Create New section of the Welcome screen.

3 Delete the temporary name, Unnamed Site 1. Enter **Banner** as the name for the new site.

● **Note:** If there is already a site named Banner, name the site something different, such as Banner2.

4 Click the Folder icon to the right of the Local Site Folder field.

The Choose Root Folder dialog box opens.

5 Browse to the Lesson12_Banner folder, open it, and select the deploy-to-web folder that was created when you published your application.

6 Click Open and then click Select/Choose.

7 Click Save.

▶ **Tip:** If the Files panel is not open, Choose Window > Files.

Your local root folder is defined. The Dreamweaver Files panel displays the folders and files for your site.

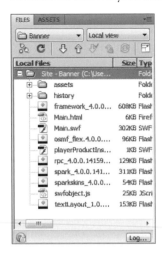

Connect to a remote site

Many websites let you publish files through FTP. You can connect to a remote site by using the Site Definition dialog box in Adobe Dreamweaver CS5.

To complete this activity, you need to have a site to which you can publish files and the FTP login information for accessing the site.

1 Choose Site > Manage Sites from the menu bar.

The Manage Sites dialog box opens.

2 Select the site named Banner (the one you just created), and click Edit.

The Site Setup dialog box opens.

3 Click Servers in the left column.

The Servers area of the Site Setup dialog box opens.

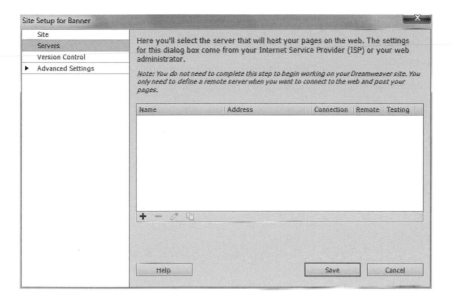

4 Click the Add Server button (**+**).

5 Enter your FTP access information.

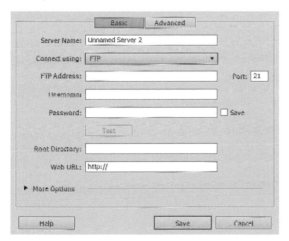

● **Note:** You can get your FTP access information from your site administrator or Internet service provider.

6 Click Test to test the connection.

Dreamweaver confirms the connection.

7 Click Save.

The new server appears in the list of servers in the Site Setup dialog box.

8 Click Save to close the Site Setup dialog box.

9 Click Done to close the Manage Sites dialog box.

Upload files

Once you establish an FTP connection, you can publish files directly from the Files panel.

1   Make sure the Dreamweaver Files panel is open.

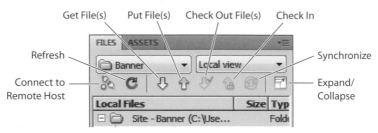

Get File(s)   Put File(s)   Check Out File(s)   Check In

Refresh

Connect to
Remote Host

Synchronize

Expand/
Collapse

2   Click the Expand/Collapse icon in the Files panel toolbar.

The Files panel expands.

3   Click the Connect To Remote Host icon to select it, if it's not already selected.

Dreamweaver connects to the web server.

4   Select the root folder for your site in the Local (right) pane.

5   Click the Put Files icon. If you are asked to confirm the file transfer, then click OK.

> **Tip:** To upload one or more folders or files without uploading the entire site, select them and click the Put Files icon.

Dreamweaver uploads the application files and opens the Background File Activity dialog box. You can save a log file with details about the file transfer.

6   Click Close to close the dialog box.

7   Click the Expand/Collapse icon to collapse the Files panel.

8   Choose File > Exit to close Dreamweaver.

Review questions

1 What are the three types of applications you can publish from your Flash Catalyst project?

2 Which two application types are published by default?

3 Why would you ever choose not to build a project for accessibility?

4 Which fonts should be embedded in the application when you publish?

5 What is an Adobe AIR application?

6 What are the main steps you need to complete when publishing an application to the web using Adobe Dreamweaver?

7 Which of the published application folders do you use as the site root folder when you upload your application to the web?

Review answers

1 You can publish three types of applications. One version includes the necessary files to run the project as a web application, but cannot run locally. A second version can run locally, but cannot be run from a web server or launch URLs. The third version is an Adobe AIR application that runs from the desktop without a browser or Internet connection.

2 Deploy-to-web and run-local are published by default.

3 Including the accessibility options when you publish a project results in a larger SWF file. You can deselect Build For Accessibility to reduce the size of your application SWF file.

4 In general, don't embed fonts if you know that users already have them. To be safe, embed any fonts other than Arial, Courier New, Georgia, Times New Roman, and Verdana. Embedding non-web fonts ensures that users see the design exactly as you do, even if they don't have the same fonts on their computer.

5 Adobe AIR is a cross-operating system runtime that allows you to build and deploy rich Internet applications (RIAs) to the desktop. Using Flash Catalyst, you can publish the project as an Adobe AIR application and then upload the published file to your web server. This allows someone to download and install the application locally. The application runs on their desktop without a web browser or an Internet connection.

6 Start Dreamweaver and create a new site. To do this, you create a local root folder and site structure. Connect to the remote site. Upload the Flash Catalyst application files.

7 The deploy-to-web folder can be used as the site root folder when publishing the application to the web using Dreamweaver.

13

EXTENDING YOUR PROJECT USING ADOBE FLASH BUILDER

Lesson Overview

Using Flash Catalyst and Adobe Flash Builder, designers and developers work together to create the perfect mix of artwork, interactivity, usability, and data. Art is joined to data, which then becomes art.

This lesson explores a few ways that you can extend your Flash Catalyst project using Flash Builder, and offers a few tips for preparing a project file (FXP) for handoff to a developer. Developing in Flash Builder goes beyond the scope of this course, but for those who have Flash Builder installed, we've included the steps to opening a Flash Catalyst project in Flash Builder, updating an existing project, and importing a Flash Catalyst project library.

In this lesson, you'll learn how to do the following:

* Extend an application by connecting it to data and web services

* Prepare the application for handoff to a developer using Flash Builder

* Import a Flash Catalyst project into Flash Builder

* Compare and integrate code between two projects

* Import a Flash Catalyst project library into Flash Builder

 This lesson will take about 45 minutes to complete. Copy the Lesson13 folder into the lessons folder that you created on your hard drive for these projects (or create it now), if you haven't already done so. As you work on this lesson, you won't be preserving the start files; if you need to restore the start files, copy them from the *Adobe Flash Catalyst CS5 Classroom in a Book* CD.

Extend the reach and functionality of your Flash Catalyst projects with Adobe Flash Builder. Create a dashboard for managing a database, searching for records, and running reports. Link a photo gallery to an unlimited portfolio of images. Collect user information, process forms, and a whole lot more.

Adobe Flash Builder

As wonderful as it is, Flash Catalyst has its limitations as a standalone RIA production tool. After all, it's an interaction design tool, not a development environment. When your application needs to retrieve data at runtime from a web server, web service, or third-party API (application programming interface), use Flash Builder.

Adobe Flash Builder 4 (formerly Flex Builder) is an integrated development environment (IDE) for developing cross-platform data-centric content. It provides features that are aimed at those who are developing RIAs using ActionScript and the Flex framework.

● **Note:** An integrated development environment (IDE) is a software application that provides comprehensive tools to computer programmers for software development.

Extending the application

Although you can use Flash Catalyst to publish fully functional applications, or microsites, many RIAs require additional development, such as binding a component to a data source or web service. That's where Flash Builder comes in. Remember, the applications you create with Flash Catalyst are Flex applications. A Flex developer can open your projects in Flash Builder and pick up right where you left off.

The following are a few examples of ways that a developer can extend the capabilities of your Flash Catalyst project using Flash Builder.

Bind components to a data source

▶ **Tip:** In addition to displaying lists of text and images, your Flash Catalyst project can be a dashboard to provide insight into a corporate database, or perhaps your application will provide a new front-end to an existing ColdFusion or PHP application.

Create a Data List component in Flash Catalyst and use design-time data to define the appearance and behavior of the list. Then, have your developer bind the component to a data source using Flash Builder. When the application runs, your data list includes every record in the data source. The data is kept separate from the application, so the data can change at any time without redesigning or republishing the application.

Using Flash Builder, you can connect the application to several service types:

- BlazeDS
- ColdFusion
- HTTP
- LCDS
- PHP
- WSDL (Web Service)
- XML

BlazeDS ColdFusion HTTP LCDS

PHP Web Service XML

Create, Read, Update, and Delete (CRUD)

Use Flash Catalyst to design a data management control center to view, edit, add, and delete records in a database. For example, you can use a wireframe Data List component to build the data grid, and then add controls to accomplish tasks, such as add new records, submit changes, or cancel. A developer can use Flash Builder to implement the CRUD functionality by binding the controls you design in Flash Catalyst to web services.

Provide a keyword search

You can connect your application to a data source and then let users search for specific records by entering keywords in a search field that you design. A developer can implement the feature using Flash Builder.

Collect user input

Flash Catalyst is an excellent tool for designing user input controls, including text input fields, radio buttons, check boxes, and the button used to submit a form. Design your forms using Flash Catalyst and then have your developer add the code to collect, store, and circulate the information by email.

Validate user input

You can assign rules to the fields in a form; determine which information is required and optional; test a password and either grant entrance or display an error message. Test the user entry in a ZIP code text input field and display an error message if the entry doesn't have exactly five numerals. These types of interactions cannot be implemented in Flash Catalyst. But you can use Flash Catalyst to design the fields and error states. The developer implements the logic for these interactions using Adobe Flash Builder.

Add a combo box

Improve the usability of a form by adding a combo box control. A combo box is a combination of a drop-down list and a single-line text input field, allowing users to either type a value directly into the control or choose from a list of existing options that you specify. You can design a combo box using a custom component, or let your developer add a combo box control using Flash Builder.

Use sliders to set values

You can use Horizontal and Vertical Slider components to select a value by moving a slider thumb between the end points of the slider track. The current value of the slider is determined by the relative location of the thumb between the end points of the slider, corresponding to the slider's minimum and maximum values. Once you add a slider in Flash Catalyst, a developer can add the desired functionality using Adobe Flash Builder.

Create printer controls

Design a print button using custom artwork in Flash Catalyst. Your developer can add the code used to initiate print commands and options.

Exploring designer-developer workflows

Technically speaking, Flash Catalyst and Flash Builder are not "integrated." However, they are designed to work together.

Every project created in Flash Catalyst can be opened in Flash Builder. A Flex developer completes the project using Flash Builder, while maintaining all the pixel-perfect layout and interactions you've designed in Flash Catalyst.

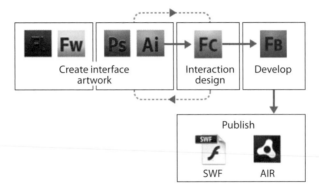

There are several possible workflows that designers and developers can use to collaborate during RIA design and development. Most fall into two general categories: linear and iterative.

Linear workflow

In a linear workflow, you will create your project in Flash Catalyst and then pass it off to the developer to use in creating the application, with little or no iteration. The following is one example of a linear workflow:

1. Create your artwork in a Creative Suite tool.

2. Import it into Flash Catalyst and use the features in Flash Catalyst to add states, animation, and interactivity.

3. Save your project as an FXP file.

4. Provide the FXP file to the person who will be responsible for implementing the additional functionality in the application. This could be yourself or a developer on the production team.

5. Import the Flex Project (FXP) file into Flash Builder.

6. In Flash Builder, define calls to remote operations that will fetch data at runtime.

7. Publish the completed project from Flash Builder.

Iterative workflow

It's possible that you'll need to make changes to the visual design of the application or its components following the export from Flash Catalyst and import into Flash Builder. But, it's not possible to re-open a Flex project in Flash Catalyst once you've imported it into Flash Builder. If you think you'll need to make changes to the artwork used in the component skins, or elsewhere in the application, you can use the following approach:

1. Open the original project file (FXP) in Flash Catalyst. Use the same file you originally imported into Flash Builder.

2. Use Save As to create a new version of the project file (FXP) using a new name.

3. Make the necessary design changes to the new project file in Flash Catalyst.

4. In Flash Builder, import the updated FXP file as a new copy of the project.

5. Copy edited code in the new project to the original project using the Flash Builder Compare feature. By comparing the original and edited projects, you can identify and copy code between projects.

Preparing files for a developer

As you design and create your Flash Catalyst project, keep in mind that you have an internal client—your Flex developer. The following tips will help you create a well-organized Flash Catalyst project that's prepared for a smooth transition into Flash Builder.

Meet with your development team early

A little planning goes a long way. When designing a Flash Catalyst project for Flash Builder, meet with your developer first to discuss which Flash Catalyst components and properties to use. If you've created a design specification, provide that to your developer along with the Flash Catalyst project file.

Use data lists and design-time data

If your application presents a list of items (images or text) from an external data source, you do not need to add every item to the component in Flash Catalyst. Instead, add a few design-time data items as a prototype. Be sure to include enough to demonstrate the desired look and behavior of the component. For example, if the list is meant to scroll, include enough data to activate the scroll bar. A nice thing about creating your data lists in Flash Catalyst is that the states of your repeated item are preserved in Flash Builder. The Normal, Over, and Selected states look and behave the same for every record.

Name everything

Use descriptive names for all layers and objects in the Layers panel. Give unique and identifiable names to all page states, components, and component states. Give all library assets unique names that your developer can recognize. Your developer will thank you for it.

Delete unused assets

In just about every project, you'll end up with at least a few unused assets. Using the Library panel in Flash Catalyst, remove any components, images, media, and optimized graphics that aren't being used in the project. The less clutter you bring into Flash Builder the better. Removing these assets also keeps your file to a more manageable size.

Opening a Flash Catalyst project in Flash Builder

Let's take a look at the main steps for getting a Flash Catalyst project into Flash Builder. We'll start by viewing a final Flash Catalyst project file (FXP) and importing the file into Flash Builder. After that, we'll import an edited version of the project and use the Compare feature to integrate the changes between the old and new projects.

Review the final Flash Catalyst project file (FXP)

A Flash Catalyst project is a Flex project. To make sure your developer is working with the most recent copy of the project file (FXP), it's always a good idea to open the file, review the elements that need further development, and resave the file before handing it over to a developer.

Let's open a finished copy of the Restaurant Guide application. We'll take a look at what needs to be completed in Flash Builder.

1   Start Flash Catalyst, browse to the Lesson13 folder on your hard drive, and open the Lesson13_Restaurants.fxp file.

2   Choose File > Run Project.

The application includes a list of restaurants. You can use the left and right scroll arrows to see more restaurants. This is a Data List component displaying design-time data. A developer can connect this to a data source, thereby extending the list to an unlimited number of restaurants stored in a database. As the restaurant information changes, the list remains current without the need to redesign or republish the application.

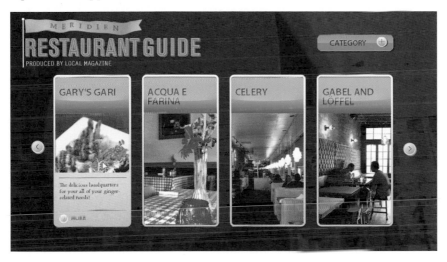

3   Click any restaurant and choose Reviews.

The application includes another data list with sample design-time customer reviews. The reviews need to be replaced by real reviews.

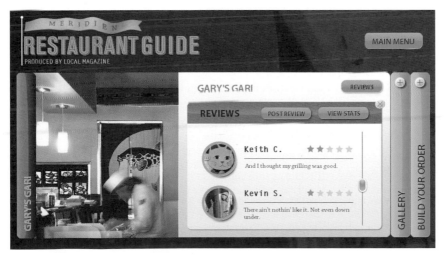

4 Click Post Review.

Nothing happens. This feature requires that users add new reviews, or records, to the database. This can be implemented using Flash Builder.

5 Click Build Your Order (on the right side of the window).

Users can fill out a form and submit their order. This feature can be implemented using Flash Builder.

6 Close the browser and return to Flash Catalyst.

Normally, you would save any last minute changes that you've made, but this file is already complete and ready to import into Flash Builder.

7 Close the project and exit Flash Catalyst.

Import the FXP into Flash Builder

To bring your design into Flash Builder, you will start Flash Builder and import the FXP file. You'll have the option to import a file or a project folder. You want to import the FXP file that you created and saved in Flash Catalyst.

You need to have Adobe Flash Builder installed to complete this exercise.

1 Start Flash Builder.

2 Choose File > Import Flex Project (FXP).

The Import Flex Project dialog box opens. The entire project is stored in a single file, so we'll leave the File option selected.

● **Note:** When importing an FXP project created with Adobe Flash Catalyst, the imported project can contain references to fonts that are not available on your system. The Import wizard provides the option to fix font references using CSS. If you select this option, Flash Builder imports the Flash Catalyst style sheet Main.css. Main.css contains references to the fonts used in the project.

3 Browse to the Lesson13 folder on your hard drive, select the Lesson13_Restaurants.fxp file, and click Open.

The path to the file is added to the dialog box. Flash Builder will create a new project and import the code and assets that Flash Catalyst generated during the interaction design phase of the project.

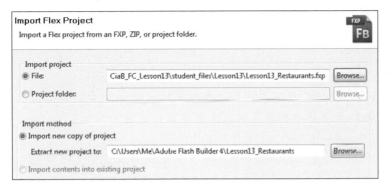

4 Click Finish.

The new Flex project is created.

5 In the Package Explorer (on the left), expand the project and then expand the src and assets folders.

The project includes any assets (graphics, images, and media) that you added to the project in Flash Builder.

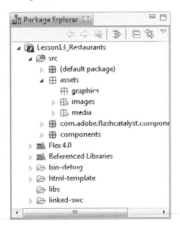

● **Note:** If you import the same FXP or FXPL file again, a new project is added with the same name, followed by the number 2. If you add it again, the name is followed by 3, and so on. To remove these files, you need to delete the project by selecting it in the Package Explorer and choosing Edit > Delete > Yes. You must also delete the project folder at the location you specified when you imported the file.

6 Expand the images folder to view the images in the project.

7 Collapse the images folder, and expand the media folder to see the media for the project.

8 Collapse the media folder, and expand the components folder to see the Flex components that were created in Flash Catalyst.

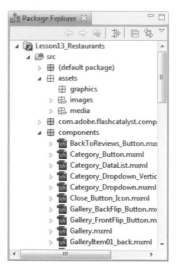

9 Collapse the components and assets folders.

10 Expand the default package folder, and double-click the Main.mxml document to open it.

You can see that Flash Catalyst was creating Flex code automatically, which is what makes this integration between applications so easy.

This is the main application file. It defines the layout for each of the states, any transitions between those states, and any interactions that you defined at the application level. This file does not contain the definition for any components that you defined within Flash Catalyst; these can all be found in the components package.

You can now use the Source and Design views in Flash Builder and the Data/Services panel to define calls to remote operations that will fetch data at runtime.

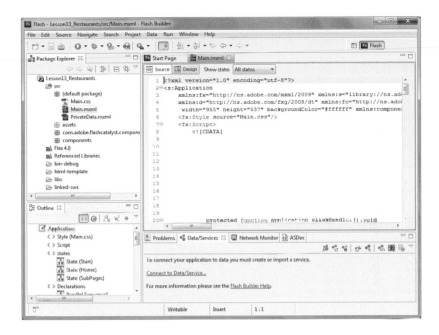

11 Choose Run > Run Main.

The Flex application runs in a browser. This should look very familiar because it's the same application you viewed from within Flash Catalyst. Notice that as you roll over the different restaurants in the list, they all have the same opacity. We've created an edited version of the application where the Normal state of the repeated item is slightly transparent, making these items appear brighter when rolling over them or when they're selected. Next, we're going to open the edited version of the application in Flash Builder and learn how to incorporate the changes from the edited project.

12 Close the browser, and close the Main.mxml document tab.

13 Keep the project open in Flash Builder for the next exercise.

Import an edited FXP file into Flash Builder

If you need to modify the artwork or interaction design in your Flash Catalyst project after working with it in Flash Builder, you'll need to create a new FXP file. Make a copy of the original Flash Catalyst project file and give it a new name. Edit the new file and import the updated FXP into Flash Builder.

For this example, we've already created an updated FXP file. Let's see what happens when you open that file in Flash Builder.

1 In Flash Builder, choose File > Import Flex Project (FXP).

The Import Flex Project dialog box opens. The File option is selected, and that's what you want.

2 Browse to the Lesson13 folder on your hard drive, select the Lesson13_Edit.fxp file, and click Open.

The path to the file is added to the dialog box. Flash Builder will create a new project and import the edited version of the code and assets.

3 Click Finish.

The new project, Lesson13_Edit, is added to the Package Explorer. With both projects open in Flash Builder, you can compare and update any code that has changed.

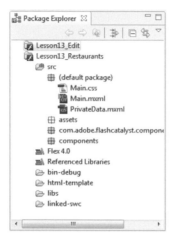

4 Leave both projects open for the next exercise.

Compare and integrate code between projects

You can use the Flash Builder Compare feature to incorporate the changes from the edited Flash Catalyst project into the original copy of the project in Flash Builder.

1 In the Package Explorer, right-click Lesson13_Edit and choose Compare Project With Version > Lesson13_Restaurants.

Flash Builder compares all the files contained within both projects and provides a list of files in which there are differences.

2 In the Structure Compare pane of the Compare tab, expand the src folder, expand the components folder, and double-click the RepeatedItem4.mxml document to open it.

The two versions of the RepeatedItem4.mxml document open side by side. The compare tool provides a visual preview of the differences between the original and the new file so that you can determine whether a change should be incorporated into the project. Any differences in the code are highlighted. In this case, the opacity in the Normal state of the repeated item has changed, as shown in Line 30 of the code.

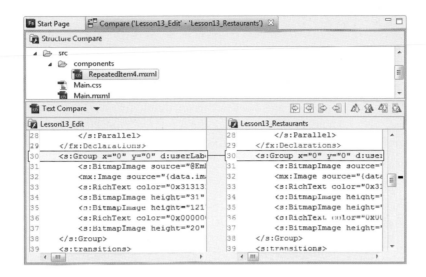

You can use the toolbar to step through the changes and to copy changed code from the left to right window, or from right to left as appropriate.

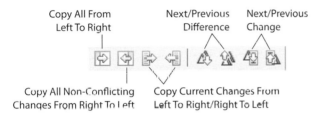

Copy All From Left To Right

Next/Previous Difference

Next/Previous Change

Copy All Non-Conflicting Changes From Right To Left

Copy Current Changes From Left To Right/Right To Left

3 Click the Copy All From Left To Right icon.

4 Close the Compare tab.

A message asks if you want to save the change you made to the code.

5 Click Yes to save the changes.

6 In the Package Explorer, double-click to open the Main.mxml file for the Lesson13_Restaurants project.

7 Choose Run > Run Main to open the project in a browser.

The edits we made in Flash Catalyst show up in the original Flash Builder project. Now the restaurants in the data list begin slightly dimmed (due to the change in opacity), and when you roll over them, they appear brighter. If you select a restaurant and then return to the Main Menu, the selected item appears brighter than the others.

8 Close the browser and return to Flash Builder.

9 Close the Main.mxml document tab.

Importing a Flash Catalyst library file (FXPL)

An FXPL contains only the component skins, item renderers, custom components, and supporting assets that you've defined in your project and not the main application MXML document. This makes the Flash Catalyst Library Package ideal for sharing a set of reuseable component designs across multiple Flash Catalyst projects and makes it possible to deliver updated sets of component skins in a single package for use in Flash Builder.

Import the FXPL

When you import a Flash Catalyst Library Package (FXPL) into Flash Builder, a Flex Library project is created. This type of project contains code that has been designed for use with one or more Flex applications.

1 In Flash Builder, choose File > Import Flex Project (FXP).

The Import Flex Project dialog box opens. The File option is selected, and that's what you want.

2 Browse to the Lesson13 folder on your hard drive, select Restaurants_library.fxpl, and click Open.

The path to the file is added to the dialog box. You have the option of importing the library as a new project or importing the contents of the library directly into an existing project.

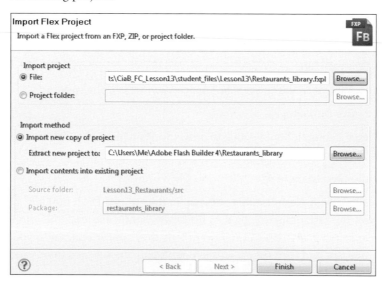

3 Click Finish to import the library package as a new Library project in Flash Builder.

The Flex Library project, Restaurants_library, is added to the Package Explorer. You can now associate this library with any existing application.

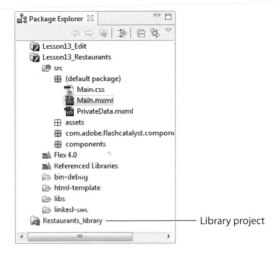
Library project

Associate the FXPL with your application

Now that you've imported the Flash Catalyst Library Package (FXPL) as a new Flex Library project in Flash Builder, you can associate the library and its assets with one or more Flex projects.

1 Select Lesson13_Restaurants in the Package Explorer and choose File > Properties.

2 Select Flex Build Path in the left pane.

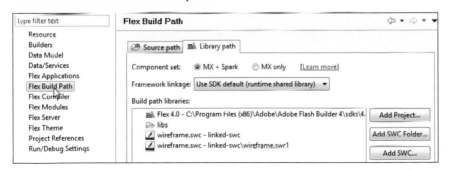

3 On the Library Path tab, click Add Project.

The Add Project Library dialog box shows any Flex Library projects you have open.

4 Select Restaurants_library and click OK.

The Restauraunts_library is added to the list of build path libraries. When you compile the application, the relevant code from the Library project will be included automatically in your compiled SWF file.

The components package containing all the component skins, as created by Flash Catalyst, is now available for use within your Flex application, and you can associate skins with appropriate components using the skinClass attribute on the component tag or in a CSS document.

▶ **Tip:** When additional component skins become available or existing skins are updated, you can import a new FXPL file and replace the existing Flex Library project. The new component skins are available within your Flex application. For this approach to work, avoid making changes to the files within the components package in Flash Builder.

Congratulations. You've reached the end of this course on Adobe Flash Catalyst CS5. We've covered a lot of information, but when you think about the potential for designing rich Internet applications using Flash Catalyst, we've really just scratched the surface.

Now it's time to take what you've learned and combine it with a little more practice and some imagination. Before you know it, you'll be quickly turning your favorite design ideas into fully functioning web and desktop applications. Have fun.

Review questions

1 What are some reasons you would bring your Flash Catalyst project into Flash Builder for further development?

2 What service types can you connect to in Flash Builder?

3 What does CRUD functionality refer to?

4 What are some things that you can do to make your Flash Catalyst file (FXP) easier to work with in Flash Builder?

5 Which file do you open in Flash Builder to run the application?

6 If you need to make changes to the Flash Catalyst document after development has begun in Flash Builder, what should you do?

7 How can you add components that you've designed in Flash Catalyst to a project in Flash Builder?

Review answers

1 Although you can use Flash Catalyst to publish fully functional applications, or microsites, many RIAs require additional development, such as binding a component to a data source or web service.

2 BlazeDS, ColdFusion, HTTP, LCDS, PHP, WSDL (Web Service), and XML.

3 Create, Read, Update, and Delete. You can use Flash Catalyst to design a data management control center used to view, edit, add, and delete records in a database. A developer can use Flash Builder to map CRUD functionality to data service calls, and then apply them to the controls you design in Flash Catalyst.

4 Use design-time data in a Data List component. Use descriptive names for pages, states, layers, and assets in the library. Delete assets from the library if they're not used in the application.

5 Open the Main.mxml file, and choose Run > Run Main.

6 Save a backup copy of the original FXP document. Edit the copy and import the copy into Flash Builder as a new project. Use the Compare feature in Flash Builder to compare changes to the code and update the project.

7 In Flash Catalyst, export the project library. Then, import the library as a new Flex Library project in Flash Builder and associate it with the application by adding it to the application's list of build path libraries.

INDEX

design documents, 12, 37–38, 39
fidelity options for, 38, 39
file size limits for, 37
images, 40
library packages, 57
sound files, 147
SWF files, 166–167
video, 147
Include Unused Symbols option, 38
information architects, 10
information resources, 5–6
installing Flash Catalyst, 2
instances, 34
best practice for using, 38
link between source files and, 50, 54
removing all for specific assets, 52–53
renaming in the Layers panel, 54
integrated development environment (IDE), 14, 242
integrating code, 252–253
interactions, 13, 90, 115–120
action sequence, 124, 138–140
built-in, 115
conditional, 116–118
deleting, 116
external link, 119–120
modifying, 116
On Application Start, 120
page navigation, 116
review questions/answers on, 121
triggering, 115
video control, 155
Interactions panel, 16, 116
interactive ads, 1, 9
interactive components. See components
interactive links, 119–120
interactive web designers, 10
Internet applications. See rich Internet applications
italicized text, 4
Item Highlight Rectangle, 187
iterative workflow, 245

K

Keep editable option, 39
keyboard shortcuts, 4
for opening projects, 19
for shape tools, 205
keyword search, 243
Knockout Drop Shadow property, 218

L

labels, button, 102
Layer Comps, 12, 31
layer folders, 62, 69
Layer Groups, 32
layers, 60–73
adding, 69
arranging, 70–71
deleting, 69
expanding/collapsing, 62–63
hiding, 36
locking/unlocking, 36, 65
naming convention for, 33
organizing artwork using, 32
overview of lesson on, 60
renaming, 63
review questions/answers on, 72–73
showing/hiding, 36, 63–64
stacking order of, 69–71, 77
Layers panel, 16, 60–73
dimmed objects in, 82, 84
editing components in, 93
grouping objects in, 66
illustrated, 62
optimizing complex groups in, 67–68
renaming objects in, 54, 66–67
stacking order in, 69–71
states viewed in, 80
lesson files, 3–4
Letterbox video option, 150
library packages
exporting, 56
importing, 57
Library panel, 16, 46–59
adding assets to, 48, 49–50
compressing images in, 53
deleting assets from, 52–53
dragging SWF files from, 166
overview of lesson on, 46
previewing files in, 51–52, 147–148
renaming assets in, 53–54
review questions/answers on, 58–59
types of assets in, 48
using assets in, 54–55
video and sound files in, 147–148
wireframe components and, 92, 94
See also project library
Line tool, 199, 207
Linear easing option, 132
linear workflow, 244–245